FAST JETS

ON THE FRONT LINE

To Wendy and James
My camp followers who came all the way

And to Monty and Miles
My dear grandsons who came later

FAST JETS
ON THE FRONT LINE

Flying Phantoms, Javelins and Tornados
in the Cold War

ALAN MUNRO

GRUB STREET • LONDON

Published by
Grub Street
4 Rainham Close
London SW11 6SS

A CIP record for this title is available from the British Library

ISBN-13: 978-1-911714-24-8

Design by Myriam Bell Design, UK
Printed and bound by Finidr, Czechia

CONTENTS

INTRODUCTION AND ACKNOWLEDGEMENTS

This tale is not about the early years. Mine were not too different from my peers; a cadet gliding course at RAF Hornchurch (long since a housing estate), then a flying scholarship on Tiger Moths at Fairoaks, followed by Chipmunks at White Waltham in the University of London Air Squadron, and then standard training on the Jet Provost and the Folland Gnat. This tale is just about flying fighters; all I ever wanted to do in the RAF. I struggled on the Jet Provost but loved the Gnat and was posted to fly the Lightning. This lasted right up to a routine visit to the RAF Valley's medical officer who took one look at my leg length, then pronounced, "I don't think so". He was right of course, and my posting was quickly changed to the Gloster Javelin, for which the operational conversion unit (No. 228) had just re-opened at RAF Leuchars in Fife, to train more crews for the Far East.

I have written at some length about the Javelin, which was well liked by its crews. In some ways, as an air-defence fighter, it was well ahead of its time and much – incorrectly in my view – has been said about it. I moved on from there prematurely – with hindsight a wrong decision – to the Central Flying School (CFS) at RAF Little Rissington to train as a Jet Provost flying instructor and spent an enjoyable two years at RAF Linton-on-Ouse, near York, instructing naval midshipmen and the occasional future admiral. Then it all went wrong.

In the unlikely event that I ever had a career, it was cancelled by the UK's withdrawal from East of Suez. I guess we saw that last of the Empire, with maybe 80 aircraft on the line at RAF Tengah most days, and that was just the fighters and bombers. After a year as a happy young flying instructor, I was called into the chief flying instructor's office after Christmas leave and asked for three choices of ground posting. It seemed that we were training too many instructors for the future reduced air force, and 40 instructors in a certain experience bracket would be grounded. There was really no answer to that, and I was one of them.

In the event we nearly all received ground postings within Training Command, with a large number to Apprentice Training Schools. To the RAF, being an officer was always more important than flying. I drew RAF Hereford, No. 3 School of Technical Training, to look after administrative apprentices. There was no airfield there and it was the RAF through a looking glass. The ground branches ruled, and I was a million miles from where I wanted to be, and eventually the solitary pilot. My career was over, with two short tours behind me and inadequate reports for promotion. I probably slid into a kind of despair that I would never see the front line again, although I was sustained by the 16 year olds who actually needed me, and I had discovered Shobdon, where I started a parallel career of flying club instructing. And of course, Hereford is one of England's great secrets as a wonderful place to live.

With my confidence totally shattered, I was eventually posted to Lightnings once again. I messed up a posting to the Harrier when this was changed, and eventually arrived at 228 Operational Conversion Unit (OCU), my spiritual home, to fly the Phantom from RAF Coningsby. In the meantime we put down roots in Rutland, some 50 years ago.

Most of this book concerns the Phantom and Air Defence. It is also a very personal reflection on the equipment and people who made up the greater RAF family in the 1970s and 1980s. My wife Wendy was a constant source of inspiration and a star when it came to proofreading. Dave Unwin, the well-known aviation journalist, was a consistent source of encouragement to get all the stories into writing and then finding a publisher for me. John Davies, publisher at Grub Street for agreeing to publish this and of course, Grub Street's editor Natalie Parker's incredible diligence has made it hopefully more readable than I managed.

Alan Munro
February 2025

PROLOGUE

"YOU'RE OPERATIONAL" – 60 SQUADRON, RAF TENGAH 1966

"Well chaps, this wasn't really how we wanted to do it. Squadron drinks, badges and so on, but we need a crew for Tramp Q1 imminently, so congratulations, you're now operational! I'll come and brief you shortly." It took a few moments to sink in. We had just landed, but this was it, the culmination of several years of training now on the other side of the world, the reason we had both joined the RAF and worked so hard to qualify. The 'Tramp' Javelins were parked almost outside the squadron, fully armed with four Firestreak infrared missiles and four 30-mm Aden cannons loaded with high explosive rounds. A fast access taxiway had been constructed so that we could accelerate onto the runway and be airborne inside a couple of minutes. We took our helmets out to the aircraft, signed the paperwork offered by the ground crew, and placed our life jackets next to the door. We then hung around trying to look busy. Our flight commander, who had declared us operational, beamed at us every time he passed by. The boss shook his head in amazement.

Tramp was the name of the quick reaction alert (QRA) pair of aircraft on readiness 24/7, with two crews at ten-minute readiness. There were bunks in the squadron and meals came from the sergeants' mess, just behind the squadron. All this went back into the Emergency when President Sukarno of Indonesia had declared his intention to annex Malaysian Borneo. This was known as the Indonesian Confrontation. No. 60 Squadron had been reinforced up to 50 aircraft at one point, including C Flight at Butterworth, the Royal Australian Air Force base opposite Penang Island. No. 64

Squadron had flown out a few years previously, and crew had rotated through Borneo, essentially Labuan, Kuching and sometimes Tawau. Fresh crews were needed which led to the temporary re-establishment of 228 OCU at RAF Leuchars to train 30 crews.

Crews were constituted and I was still with Chris Donovan. I think we were as surprised as the boss that we had gone from unqualified to Q1 in a matter of minutes, and we never did get the promised briefing. The speaker in our little operations room, with an open line to RAF Bukit Gombak, the fighter control radar station in the middle of Singapore, erupted. "Tramp, Tramp, Tramp. Crews to cockpit." This was it. We just grabbed our life jackets, ran for the aircraft, vaulted a monsoon drain and strapped in. Both aircraft were connected by telebrief, an open line also to Bukit Gombak, and here was the controller passing us a scramble order, one aircraft only. Two splayed fingers on both start buttons, and the engines fired up. Since the starter was driven by AVPIN, a form of nitro-glycerine, one at a time was the norm, but we were in a hurry. Later we heard tales about the boss taking a particularly old and offensive officer's hat, chucking it into a metal civil service wastepaper bin with a pint of AVPIN, and throwing in a match. The hat was incinerated, the bin was wrecked and there was bad blood between the boss and the hat's owner forever afterwards.

This time both engines fired up, chocks away and we were accelerating towards the fast access track as air traffic control passed a take-off clearance. We must have cornered at about 80 knots and were quickly airborne accelerating to 450 knots for the climb. Afterburners in at 12,000 feet, climbing speed now Mach 0.9, and then levelling at around 25,000 feet on instruction from fighter control and heading up the Malacca Straits. At 20 miles Chris acquired a radar contact and set us up for a stern conversion. The mission had been passed as 'Identify'. Well, no problems there; we just didn't arm up. It was an RAF Canberra returning from the north with no flight plan. We never did find out why, and when we saw the pilot later, he wasn't talking.

Phew! Job done, pulse rates back to normal and adrenalin surge over. We landed and taxied back to the squadron, handed the aircraft over to the ground crew and signed in. And there was our flight commander leaning against the door. "Not bad. A bit slow on the start, but you made up for it on the corners. Here are your squadron badges. Get them sewn on please." Yes, we were pretty pleased with ourselves, but after a night in the bunks and no breakfast, we'd calmed down. This was our first Cold War, there was still an air threat to Singapore, and we started to take it all quite seriously. We had arrived.

CHAPTER ONE

THE JAVELIN

NO. 228 OCU, RAF LEUCHARS, JANUARY 1966

"You're posted to Lightnings." Phew, got there! The top of the Gnat course went to Lightnings, and that was our dream. Incidentally the bottom of the course went to Vulcans, strange as that may now seem, but we dreaded it. The Gnat training was going well. My wife Wendy – to whom I got married in 1964, straight from university – and I had moved to a summer holiday home in Trearddur Bay, and she was teaching in a school there. We loved living in Anglesey and Bob Turner, my South African instructor, had taught me to love flying the Gnat. What could go wrong? I went to the doctor.

I had a nasty cold as winter approached, and in those days, it was obligatory to see the quack. He duly issued a sick note saying something like 'No flying for 48 hours'. Then he asked me about our course postings and looked up when I said Lightnings. "I'm not sure about that," he said and got out his early version of an ergonomics handbook, as well as a tape measure. "Not a chance," he said, "Your legs are far too long." He wrote out another sick note, and I passed both to our squadron commander.

The RAF acted swiftly in this case, and very quickly my posting had been changed to Javelins, the same air-defence role, and the conversion unit had just re-opened. Fair enough, we were off to Scotland. However, the RAF had also awarded all Javelin postees an additional ten-hour low-level high-speed training course. For this we had a dedicated instructor and a great time flying low-level cross-countries at 420 knots, a previously unknown speed for a student. We forgot all about Lightnings.

So, we rented a van, and decamped in a small bungalow in St Andrews. Javelin training didn't start until March so I was able to persuade the St Andrews University Air Squadron to let me hang out with them, and do some useful Chipmunk flying. I even managed a flight in a Lightning T.5 from 23 Squadron. I barely squeezed under the instrument panel, so I guess the doctor had been right. That Lightning

Author and Chris Donovan.

now sits in the Newark Air Museum. Our future navigators were already hard at work learning how to use the Javelin radar, mounted in Canberra T.11s (the ones with the radar nose), so that an instructor could sit side-by-side with a student. I learnt later that some people were able to play with the radar contact and turn behind a target at exactly the right moment. Others would always need little notes of the intercept geometry. We never should forget that the radar blip weighed 20 tonnes.

Compared to the Gnat, the Javelin was a massive aircraft and maybe a little scary. First, though, we had to be kitted up with the right equipment, which meant a few days at the Aviation Medicine Training Centre at RAF North Luffenham in Rutland, so we departed with the navigators and strict instructions to be 'crewed up' by the time we got back. It was actually pretty interesting. The two main aims were a 25,000-feet anoxia demonstration and then pressure breathing at an equivalent altitude of 55,000 feet. We were issued with oxygen masks, G suits and pressure jerkins that would inflate automatically to stop chest injury as oxygen was forced down the throat at 70-mm Hg pressure. All this would happen automatically if there should be a sudden cabin pressure loss at altitude.

The anoxia run was fun. Everyone had a clipboard and was given a simple task by the doctor as the air was pumped out of the chamber. Mine was to keep subtracting seven from a million. Easy. Each oxygen supply was in turn disconnected by the doctor and then reconnected after a few minutes. I found I had scribbled all over the paper when I was convinced that I was doing normal subtraction. Eventually the chamber was brought 'down' to ground level, where once off oxygen, the smell of fart was overpowering. The doctor explained this was normal.

On the first evening, a run into Stamford was obligatory, with the elephant in the room that we had to crew up. It was a little like a village hall dance where pilots and navs mingled. We went to The George. Then on the second evening we went to The Crown. Pilots stood at one end, and navs at the other. "Do you fancy the little one with the moustache?" Eventually someone proposed, followed by an undignified rush until the last two crewed up from necessity.

I crewed with Chris Donovan, with whom I had a successful partnership until I moved on. Chris actually left the RAF a few years later and built up a very successful car dealership. Then he was bought out, but he rejoined the RAF where we met again in Germany. Then very sadly, he died of cancer in his 40s. Some years after the crewing evening, I was taking out a mortgage in the Stamford Abbey National on a hot summer's day. The manager asked if I fancied a pint. He then marched to The

Crown with the papers under his arm and we signed the mortgage deeds at the same spot where Chris and I had made our contract years earlier.

Back in the classroom the doctor drew pictures of the intestines and the areas where potato crisps and Ruddles County (the infamous local ale) would produce gas which would expand very painfully in the 'big bang' to 55,000 feet. It seemed that the nearest Ruddles pub was The Fox and Hounds in North Luffenham village, so of course we all went there. The next morning, we were taken up to 25,000 feet, and then we were sealed into a smaller chamber. Air was evacuated from a third small chamber until a membrane broke and the air rushed out. The pressure breathing started where instead of breathing in and letting the chest muscles expel the air, oxygen was forced into the throat and lungs and you had to expel it forcibly. The Ruddles and crisps never stood a chance in comparison.

Back to Leuchars, and into ground school where we learnt the Javelin systems, then into the first-generation simulator for aircraft emergencies and the chance to learn how to work together. After a couple of dual flights in the Javelin T.3 (the dual-control version based on a much earlier Javelin variant), I was off with Chris in the FAW.9, the actual combat aircraft. Part of the trip was to go supersonic, starting at 45,000 feet and I do remember pointing vertically downwards watching the needle of the Machmeter quivering just under the Mach. Then just as I was about to tell him that we were supersonic (he had no Machmeter in the back), we were through, with the needle reading Mach 1.1. Big deal. The lesson learnt was not to bother. The aircraft has sat for years in the Yorkshire Air Museum at Elvington, although I read that it has moved somewhere for restoration to its former beauty.

We spent a lot of flight time at high level. The Far Eastern threat was apparently the Tupolev Tu-16 'Badger' flying at 40,000 feet, but in the end, we switched to low level. An Indonesian C-130 had apparently crashed into the Malacca Straits after being intercepted at low level by a Javelin, in the night, so this was perceived to be an additional threat. Both the very high and very low extremities of the envelope were difficult. The rest was apparently too easy to bother about. All the training involved transmitting the entire crew conversion for a staff navigatior on the ground to judge, with the ancient wartime ritual of night flying supper to follow, actually a full Scottish breakfast at six o'clock in the morning, followed by a lifetime addiction to brown sauce.

It was over all too soon. Chris and I were posted to 60 Squadron at RAF Tengah in Singapore. I said goodbye to my newish bride since we were still under 25 with no rites of passage. Transport to the Far East was a 36-hour flight in a British Eagle

Britannia from Heathrow, with refuelling stops at Abadan in Iran, and Columbo in Ceylon. There was no danger of jet lag. And then we had arrived, and I still remember the first sticky smell of the Far East as we made our way from Paya Lebar Airport, Singapore Civil, to RAF Tengah, and the start of a great new adventure.

60 SQUADRON AND THE JAVELIN

No new crews had been trained on the Javelin since 1961. Replacements were needed, especially as at the time there was no end in sight to the Indonesian Confrontation in Borneo. By the time we arrived in 1966, most of the Javelin crews had done tours in Germany and in the UK. We arrived on 60 Squadron fresh faced and full of energy and total ignorance to unguarded stares of disbelief. Those of us who had arrived via university were already flight lieutenants, when they would all previously have been one or two ranks lower. We had a lot to prove although nobody was so unkind as to say so.

It took at least three weeks to acclimatise to the hot weather, even after buying new lightweight uniforms in Tengah Village. 'Charles, Tailor of Style' (Charley's to us) and 'Heckell and Jeckell' would produce serviceable uniforms overnight, if necessary, as well as selling you cameras, hi-fis, LPs and rice cookers. One pilot's dad, who had made Huntley & Palmers biscuits his life's work, discovered a large tin of them in Charley's that had been sent out to the Suez Canal Zone in the mid-1930s. He bought them. Amazingly about half the biscuits were still edible. Both tailors had sweatshops behind the open front where a dozen local women slaved all day over sewing machines. Air conditioning was almost unknown, and there were always ice-cold cokes available to ensure customer loyalty. Laundry? Yes of course. Every day the Chinese laundry on base hung out around 300 shirts and shorts. Incredibly, nobody ever had the wrong items delivered back the next day.

After a quick dual check in the Javelin T.3 (guns only, no air intercept radar and no afterburner), we were thrown very quickly into squadron daily training, and I clearly remember on my first pairs formation take-off in a 60 Squadron Javelin FAW.9, seeing my leader's underside as the wheels came up and he split the formation into a combat spread below 100 feet. The rationale was that the high threat was an Indonesian P-51 Mustang lurking in the overhead. In reality this made no sense with 70-odd aircraft lined up in precise lines all over the airfield, as well as the RAF Regiment's anti-aircraft guns defending the perimeter. On the other hand, it felt good, and we loved it.

Monday morning air combat training four-ship climb-out.

The Javelin climb was an exciting 450 kts/M 0.9, and afterburner was selected at around 12,000 feet. This was a great joke amongst non-Javelin pilots that the aircraft lost thrust with afterburner at low level. This was quite true, in that when the burners were added to the Armstrong Siddeley Sapphire engines, return fuel was used to power them. The second law of thermodynamics (entropy etc.) ensured a three per cent power loss. There was massive spare power at low level so this really wasn't missed. There was just no point in selecting afterburner. The other cause of great amusement was centre-line closure, whereby large rain droplets might cause the turbine shroud to contract onto the turbine and seize the engine. This had happened a few times, and the quick fix was a layer of carborundum paste around the turbine to grind down the blades. It seemed to work. And unquestionably when a Javelin spun, it was unwilling to recover when the tail was blanked off by the Delta wing. However, on a couple of occasions the navigator had ejected and the reaction had forced the aircraft nose down, thus breaking the spin. It was a man's aircraft without question.

We were quickly introduced to high-level air combat, reminiscent of the Korean War. The Mk 9 Javelin could sustain a 2-G turn at 40,000 feet and the afterburner could be happily selected and deselected. The Firestreak missiles were in range at a couple of miles, although gun shots were encouraged. The problem was that nobody

A Javelin and Meteor at RAAF Butterworth during an armament practice camp.

was obliged to engage us at high level and at lower levels we were very susceptible to low-wing loaders, like 20 Squadron's Hunters, who just had to wait for us to descend. The Americans finally successfully solved this mismatch in Vietnam with high energy manoeuvring. One thing the Javelin could do though was to slow down. It possessed four airbrakes each the size of a bedroom door, and fully variable like a throttle. They were limited to half travel at 420 kts when they would provide a 1-G horizontal deceleration. You could arrive at three miles finals at 40,000 feet, dive with full airbrake and join the circuit at 1,000 feet.

In fact, for its time the Javelin was an amazing aircraft. The radar would normally see a target at around 20 miles, there was a primitive but effective IFF (transponder) interrogator, and the armament of four 30-mm Aden cannons and four Firestreaks was imposing. At low level the radar altimeter was steady enough to allow maximum rate turns at 500 feet at night during low-level intercepts, good enough to intercept an Indonesian C-130 and cause it to crash into the sea. The radar shone a target dot onto a second reflector sight for gun usage at night or in cloud.

The first serious challenge was the navigation radar leader (the NURL –head navigator and deputy boss) saying: "We're going up to Butterworth tomorrow and you'll have the boss as your No. 2." That was scary enough, but in the morning, this turned into a three-aircraft flight. I had never led a threesome, but the NURL assured me that it would all be fine. Most of it was, until we were joined by two more Butterworth Javelins as we approached Penang. I was now leading a five-ship, which all those years ago was really frightening. I managed to get the formation onto a runway approach heading and then into echelon for a break into the circuit. I never spotted the crosswind, until it was obvious that I was being blown through the runway. "I'm going round." From the back, "Keep turning". "I have to go around." "Keep turning." In the event I got the wings level a few feet before touchdown and we landed. Then as we taxied in the NURL said "See those lines of Aussie Sabres? See the squadron of Aussie Canberras? See all our Javelins?" "I'd sooner die than go around in front of them." He nearly did, but I kept quiet.

The next trip north was for air-to-air gunnery at Butterworth, firing at a flag target towed by a Meteor on a 60-mile tow. We fired two guns as a pair, with one aircraft diving to attack the flag as the other came off. I was drawn with the boss, who gradually seemed less frightening when his scores were similar to mine. The Australians had kept the five o'clock swill going for happy hour where the Sikh barman filled up a cake stand full of very small beer glasses with a rubber hose, and the trays kept circulating. The tradition was that this was the best way to drink as much beer as possible between five and six p.m., when the Australian bars were open. The idea was to force people to go home sober and it was a total failure. The RAAF loved it as a piece of New World tradition.

Back in Singapore, we gradually built up our fledgeling experience. To get to the east of the island and over the South China Sea, there was a transit route at 500 feet around the south of the harbour, returning at 1,000 feet. This allowed gun firing into the sea for operational turnrounds, when the armourers would leap onto the wings before the aircraft even came to a halt, ripping open the ammunition tanks to reload the guns with time-expired ammunition. They would load up two missiles then download them again, to simulate a full upload, all this while refuelling and re-oiling took place. The crew stayed put, grateful for the pints of orange squash that Josie, our most unwarlike coffee girl, brought out to the aircraft. The whole turnround took seven minutes, then we were taxiing once again for a repeat performance.

In the first year we also had the opportunity to fire a Firestreak missile. It needed a heat source to complete its firing circuits, so a 45 Squadron Canberra obliged by dropping a parachute flare seven miles ahead. Again, the firing range was over the South China Sea, where I got to fire my first missile. Intercept training by day and night were our bread and butter, but there was always the occasional RN aircraft carrier for practice against their Buccaneers, and maybe a quick carrier approach before returning to base after working with the Gannet AEW.3s and the navy fighter controllers. When HMS *Victorious* was in the Singapore dockyard in the Straits of Johor, the deployment ended with a magnificent cocktail party, where the bar ran the entire length of the hangar deck. The Royal Marine band came down into the party on an aircraft lift and staged a nostalgic tattoo. And finally, when it was time to go, there indeed was another bar stretching down the other side of the hangar. The navy really knew how to entertain.

RAF Tengah was an air force in itself. There were two flying wings, Air Defence with ourselves and 64 Squadron plus the Rock Ape Triple A. Rock Apes is still the mainly affectionate name for the RAF Regiment after their wartime defence of Gibraltar. It is incredible to think that at the end of the Second World War there were 400 Rock squadrons. The few highly professional airfield defence squadrons are now being cut back to be replaced by auxiliaries, but I digress. RAF Tengah's Strike Wing consisted of 20 Squadron with two dozen Hunters, 45 Squadron with Canberra bombers, 81 Squadron, half size with reconnaissance Canberras and 14 (RNZAF) Squadron with more Canberra bombers. Additionally, there was a detachment of Vulcan B.2

Wendy on board HMS *Victorious* whilst docked at Singapore dockyard being shown the landing sight.

A Fairey Gannet AEW.3 on board HMS *Victorious* which was docked at Singapore dockyard.

heavy bombers. In the circumstances that seemed to deter the Indonesians quite successfully, while they were doing their best to crash their MiG-21s.

This was surely the last shout of the Raj. Despite Singaporean independence being a year old, the British influence was still everywhere, and we really did carry on as if Singaporean and Malaysian independence was yet to happen. The Far East Air Force was one of the last great independent commands. RAF Seletar had the tactical transports, and RAF Changi had the heavies (Shackletons, Hastings, Argosies and a squadron of RNZAF Bristol Freighters), also the RAF hospital. No. 60 Squadron maintained a large C Flight at RAAF Butterworth, and there were fighter control radars at Bukit Gombak in Singapore and on Penang Island. There was nothing on the east coast of Malaysia of course. Air defence is as ever reactive to a threat, and of course there was no threat from the East. Was there?

The sun was never going to set, until it did. That was when the Wilson government closed down all military basing east of Suez. In those far off days the Defence Bill dwarfed social services, which was not regarded highly. People had emerged from the war and were just more self-sufficient. Now the situation is reversed, while the military struggles to justify its existence.

The moving finger writes.

WHAT HAPPENED TO 60 SQUADRON?

This is the saga of the RAF's squadron numbers. In the interests of tradition, one might hope that a squadron number would stick with an aircraft's role, but instead it has become almost a game. For example, when a new tanker squadron was created the number might well have been 214, the original Alan Cobham refuelling unit; not to be. Instead, it was named after the RAF's Comet squadron.

When 60 Squadron was due to be disbanded with the withdrawal from Singapore, at the same time the RAF Germany transport support squadron was due to get a number. No. 60, with colours, silver and photo albums, was duly conferred. In time 60 became a helicopter squadron and is now a helicopter training squadron manned partly by civilians. It is an emotive subject making tradition difficult.

JUNGLE SURVIVAL. RAF CHANGI, OCTOBER 1966

We were sent over to the east end of Singapore Island to the fabled RAF Changi. In the 1960s, the place had recovered from the war, the village was prosperous and the officers' mess was magnificent. The airfield itself was the home of the RAF's heavies, plus a Meteor target facilities flight, manned largely by elderly Poles. Jacaranda trees predominated and a Spitfire was mounted where it could be seen from all around. There was a single runway (still in use) and a large concrete apron for visiting aircraft (also still there). It was additionally the home of the Far East Air Force Survival and Parachute School.

This course involved a week of classroom study, including sampling just about everything that the jungle might have to offer including snake (yes, it does taste like chicken). There was even a beach day building a beach oven, then, leaving the fish and a very fresh chicken to cook. (The chicken had been running around a few minutes previously.) This was followed by a week in the jungle in mainland Malaysia. In the 1960s much of Singapore Island was still pristine jungle, as was the whole of Malaysia.

Week Two saw the course embussed with packs constructed from the gear that would be carried in an ejection seat survival pack, or whatever any individual course member might expect. All that was missing was the treescape, 200 feet of nylon cord which you buttoned onto your flying suit under the life jacket. It was quite conceivable that one might come to rest in the jungle canopy and a metal clutch could be used to lower oneself to the ground quite gently. We were going into the jungle in slightly unrealistic teams of eight or so with the leader armed with a service revolver. We thought that it was for shooting wild animals. The staff said it was for dealing with mutineers.

It was a pretty good course in fact. We very quickly learnt not to use wood that had already been chopped down (disbelievers crashed in the middle of the night), how to build shelters from parachute silk and nylon cord, how to light fires, how to march in a straight line and how to extract drinkable water. In fact, the jungle started to become quite friendly and by the end we had no fear of having to survive there. We never did see any wildlife except for one flying fox and one water snake, but the monkeys were audible all around. We started to leave OXO cubes for them tightly wrapped in silver foil which, judging from the noise, drove them crazy trying to get at the food. We marched on a compass bearing 100 paces at a time, when the second in line would shout, "Ton up". The third in line would then notch a piece of wood, and this counting was surprisingly accurate. The stick was led by a machete man who cleared the way ahead. Now our stick had picked up two Vietnamese pilots who only wanted to wield their machetes, so they led. Amazingly they never chopped each other.

In addition to my pack, I was carrying an ultra-high frequency (UHF) radio beacon which I set off at a certain time in the evening. A squadron Javelin equipped with a device called Violet Picture then arrived to home onto the signal. Actually, this system was installed to allow us to home onto a bomber that might be jamming, a technique used by the Luftwaffe in the Second World War. The idea was to offset the needle so that overflight of the beacon would be seen. The Javelin pilot would then fly through a tight 270 degrees, to pass over the beacon again. On the ground as soon as the fighter was heard homing in a second time a 'jungle rocket'[1] was fired through the tree canopy giving the fighter crew a fix on the survivor (me). It worked brilliantly but was never used operationally.

After a few days we emerged onto a jungle road. There stood two grinning locals on bicycles fitted with glass boxes. They were selling pineapple chunks and ice cream and sold out within a few minutes. How they knew we would be there was a mystery as we didn't know ourselves. An RAF coach was parked a mile away on a bridge, with the bags we had packed with essentially clean clothes. Everyone stripped off and dived in the river, long before the days of female aircrew. Then for the highlight of the

---

1 The jungle rocket was a fairly hefty bullet in a tube that fired up through the tree canopy and exploded like a big red firework; hard to miss.

week a single-engine Pioneer aircraft flew along the river and dropped a large parcel of Tiger beer cans, for which we had all paid a dollar a can. Since no-one had secured the parachute lanyard, the package crashed onto the ground and the survivors stared at the aircraft in disbelief. Then there was a rush for ammunition and the Pioneer disappeared in a hail of jungle rockets and two-star red flares; just friendly fire, and thankfully everyone missed.

So, because of the beer can disaster, the staff had the coach stop at a jungle village bar. Once everyone was settled and happy, a staff instructor walked in, reached onto his fly, and flicked two blood gorged leeches onto the floor. He then stamped on them, blood went everywhere, and the waitress fainted. The course ended with a day out in the Straits of Johor practising dinghy drill supported by an RAF Marine Branch air-sea rescue launch. A Whirlwind helicopter from RAF Seletar arrived to haul each sea survivor back onto the launch, but the water was warm, and people just dived back in and carried on.

The next day we returned to base, with the pilot from 28 Squadron (Hong Kong Hunters) checking on his one-inch fighting ant which he intended to have made into a paperweight. It never survived the journey though and emerged from its jungle rocket tube curled up and quite dead. Chris and I also turned down the chance of parachuting from the back of an Argosy into the sea. A little survival goes a long way.[2]

LIVING IN THE SUNSET

Wendy and I had committed, in the RAF's eyes, the sin of marriage under the age of 25. Money was tight, housing was difficult, and training had not been easy. However, more junior officers were arriving from university, where marriage after a degree was not uncommon. Some years later, pay and conditions were completely redesigned as a part of Denis Healey's Military Salary, but not before Wendy had been reduced to tears at the MoD when she tried to get a passage out to Singapore. Half an hour earlier the army had started to process a free ticket for her before realising that I was RAF. Nasty signals were exchanged, stretching loyalty just a little, and I had to find scarce money quickly to buy her a seat on a trooping flight. She and several other wives gradually arrived to the further horror of the older pilots. Then I had my

[2] I should add that a few years previously an army Auster pilot had left Butterworth as night was falling to fly back to Singapore. Despite an extensive search the aircraft was never seen again. The pilot, however, walked out of the jungle three weeks later unscathed. That was another lesson. Follow a stream and it will take you to a river, then eventually the sea. It worked.

25th birthday and everything changed when we suddenly had some spare dollars. We bought a massive hi-fi in a teak cabinet. As you did.

However, living did not have to be expensive, providing that you lived like a local and used their shops and market stalls. Food from the *makanan*[3] stalls was nutritious and cost just a few cents. Clothes were ridiculously cheap, and madam could afford a new dress any time she liked. Cars went forever in the warmth, even as they rusted to bits. My MGA had the registration 'SU52' which drew a small crowd when I stopped for petrol "Very Lucky". That came later. The most effective transport was without doubt the yellow and black 'pick-up taxi' which ran like a bus with fare stages. It was not uncommon to find yourself sitting next to a piglet in a basket. We were fascinated by Chinese funerals, and we attended Chinese New Year, where chopsticks were obligatory.

Change Alley, near the Singa Pura river, was the source of the more expensive electrical goods, but just when you thought you had a bargain you got home to find that the serial number had been filed off. At the time the population of the island was about 1 million, compared to 6.5 million today. Air conditioning was virtually unknown, The Jurong industrial park was a dream in the prime minister's eyes, and much of the island was still jungle. Sentosa Island was called Blakang Mati, where the Gurkhas lived, and you visited by invitation. The police had enlisted retiring soldiers into the Police Reserve and the locals were terrified of them. Even then though, things were on the move. The old Chinatown remained as just a few streets with three families still sharing a room with a several opium dens at ground level. Lee Kuan Yew was Singapore's prime minister. He had a dream, still unfolding, to make Singapore the best country in the world, long after the British had gone.

With a car, everything did change. There were some very pleasant days out to be had just over the causeway in Malaysia, and we drove all the way to Penang following signs to somewhere called 'Orantan'. Only after missing a turning and going all the way round a roundabout, did we see that 'Sudantan' was in the opposite direction. From Penang we took the train to Bangkok from Penang's railway station with no railway. You bought a ticket and got on a boat over to a mainland station. We later managed a flight to Hong Kong for a week, then got a free flight back in an Argosy from RAF Kai Tak, stopping at Labuan Island in Borneo. While we waited for the aircraft to be refuelled, we watched the door of the officers' mess hut flapping in the breeze. The building had so recently been buzzing with life and activity. In a way the place was symbolic of the eventual total British withdrawal.

---

3 Simply the Malay word for food, but it covered everything from toasties to what they called 1,000-year-old eggs.

ALL THAT JAZZ

A Hunter pilot on 20 Squadron, Dave Willis, was an expert clarinet player, who wanted to form a jazz band within the Tengah officers' mess. I must have admitted that I had played a banjo at school and straightaway he had lent me his and showed me how to tune it as a tenor. That's when the hard work started. The others he recruited were Keith, a Javelin pilot and school trumpet player, Mick, a Kiwi navigator on double bass, Pete, a Javelin pilot on drums, and Dai, a fighter controller from RAF Bukit Gombak on trombone. Then because the offer was too good to miss, Bob joined on saxophone, a Javelin pilot who had previously been a professional in the QE2 dance orchestra. We were probably awful, but since we played 'interval and afterwards' nobody minded too much.

Also, of course, as an officers' band, money could never change hands, so we played for free beer. On occasion the stage was awash with full pints as our day job colleagues realised that when they ordered eight pints, that meant seven for the band and one for themselves. However, improve we did, and it became a social accolade to have the band creep up on a weekend party and strike up on the lawn. On occasion that meant driving down the Bukit Timah Road in three sports cars, wives driving, with the band playing jazz. We even busked outside an officers' mess Tramps Ball. It was interesting watching the reactions as people arrived. Some listened for a bit and threw a few coins in the hat, some paid up and passed by totally embarrassed, some pretended we were not there, and others even turned round and took the back way into the mess. When most people had arrived, we counted the takings. We were 30 cents short of a pint each, so Dave insisted that we busked on until we had the right amount. So much for officers not playing for money.

Then two major changes took place. It was time to give the fighter controllers some flying experience and generally get together. I flew with a flight sergeant called Ken Curl, who really did not enjoy the experience. He was not just airsick, and I gradually realised that he was passing out in the back seat. Well, the Javelin had a canopy system with both Perspex bubbles attached to the same rails. Should either crew member eject themselves from the aircraft then explosive bolts would blow the entire canopy system away from the aircraft. That meant that it was quite safe to fly with the canopy open, and in this case, it probably saved Ken. We landed with an open cockpit and an ambulance waiting at the far end of the Tengah runway. After we stopped, Ken was quickly pulled out by the firemen and rushed off to the sick bay.

After the aircraft was towed back to the squadron, paperwork completed and the boss satisfied, I went to see Ken. He was sitting up still suffering from heat exhaustion and as we chatted, he asked about the band. It turned out that he had been Ken Colyer's banjo and guitar player but could never earn enough to subsist. Would we like him to coach the band? Oh yes please, and after that he never missed a Wednesday band call.

Then, on a couple of occasions we met up with the Far East Air Force Jazz Band. It seemed that the professional bands encouraged their musicians to have a second line of music, be it palm court orchestra or string quartet. This developed them as musicians. In this case we met a full-throated jazz group under the leadership of a flight sergeant trombonist called Shakespeare, just the one name that everyone called him. Since we played intervals, his idea was that as we changed over, we should do a couple of numbers together. For us that meant playing face to face with our opposite number who would coach as he played. The noise from two bands must have been incredible.

Fast forward 20 years, and as I walked out into the twilight from the Whitehall MoD, the commissionaire bawled out, "Good Night Saah". "Good Night." Then, "You don't remember me, do you Saah?" I didn't even need to look round. "Hello Shakespeare, are you still playing?" "Oh, you do remember me?" "Could I ever forget?" We chatted for maybe half an hour. He had a group in north London and would play on as long as his lungs lasted; a great musician, and an inspiration to an entire generation, us included.

AFTER CONFRONTATION, 1967

The Indonesian Confrontation ended formally on 11 August 1966. The writing was on the wall for the Javelin. Our C Flight at RAAF Butterworth was disbanded, the V bombers left (with an amazing hat-lifting flypast) and the New Zealanders went home. The jazz band lost its double bass player. 60 Squadron put on a dawn flypast over the Kranje War Memorial, an arrowhead of five aircraft coming out of the rising sun. And while all this was happening, we could sometimes hear on the UHF emergency radio frequency of 243.0 MHz the 'beep beep beep' when an ejection seat was activated in Vietnam. We were horribly conscious that as our Cold War ended, there was another increasingly hot war just a few hundred miles away over the South China Sea. Still, the fun went on.

We had another weapons detachment to RAAF Butterworth. Our dear polo-playing flight commander had long since picked up the soubriquet of 'couldn't run a piss-up in a brewery'. The expression was brand new and then little used otherwise. After flying ended one day around lunchtime, he ordered everyone into a coach which he had arranged, which then took us to the Fraser and Neave soft drinks factory. The manager was a polo friend, and we duly trudged round the bottling plant making appreciative noises. Then with one room to go here was a bar dispensing Tiger Beer in large bottles just as fast as it could be drunk. "I didn't mention that we also bottle Tiger, did I?" said the manager. As you can imagine, that took care of the afternoon, and as we fell back onto the coach, our flight commander put his head in the door with "Well, I'm off to dinner now, but don't forget to tell your friends that I was the one who organised a piss-up in a soft drinks factory!" Roger that.

This time we sent 50 boxes of Tiger cans down to Singapore in four Javelins. Apparently in the days of the Malayan Emergency, troops up country never had the opportunity to enjoy a tin while they would try to make up for it back in Singapore. That led to rationing only in Singapore, which had never been rescinded. One box fitted exactly into an ammunition tank, of which there were eight. That's 32 boxes sorted. Then several large fuselage panels took a box each and the 50 boxes had vanished. The anticipated all ranks party would not run dry. However, back in Singapore only 46 boxes were unloaded. Two weeks later, just before the party, a box was found in an aircraft undergoing hangar servicing, leading quickly to the other three. The aircraft, in the meantime had been boiled in the sunshine, frozen at high altitude then boiled again several times with the beer on board. These special Tiger cans were offered separately from the others in the event and not one person could detect the difference. I think we switched to Anchor after that.

We flew back with the undercarriage down after the engineers discovered that over the years in the rain and sun the wing wiring looms had decayed. A Javelin had landed with a wheel stuck up and numerous other wing electrical problems could be explained. We had to land and refuel courtesy of Qantas at Kuala Lumpur and got back to Tengah in time for the evening thunderstorm. "You are diverted to Changi." On arrival, an Argosy had just requested clearance. They asked us for our endurance. "Seven minutes," replied my leader, "Five minutes," from me. Just as they started to pass the transports clearance, my leader's radio radioed, "That's till the engines quit". "ASCOT, hold your position." (i.e. STOP.) We laughed.

Chris and I took part in a flight to Gong Kedah to visit our Strike Wing. This was a wartime Japanese strip, on the east end of the Thai border. The maps were incomplete and coloured white, so after flying around southern Thailand, we spotted a pair of Hunters and followed them in. The Hunter ground crew decided that we needed a replacement tyre, and one was duly arranged to be put on a Beverley leaving Singapore later in the day. We went to the beach, lazed around, swam and chatted with the fishermen. Boys ran up the coconut trees from time to time and, for a few cents, cut down coconuts for us.

When we got back, everything was running late, and we were finally ready to leave at dusk. As we rolled down the runway air traffic were extinguishing paraffin flares, and after we got airborne the radio failed. We had intended to file that flight plan once airborne. A disaster was in the making. Between us and Singapore was a civil airway extending to 45,000 feet and we decided to climb over it. Chris was sitting over our coconuts and could only talk about what might happen to his masculinity if they exploded. Then once over, we could see the thunderstorms over Singapore, this

A combined island flypast from 60 and 64 Squadrons following the disbandment of 64 Squadron.

time over the entire island. Then, as we were contemplating our immediate future, we heard a call on out emergency radio: "If you are receiving me then you are diverted to Paya Lebar." That was Singapore civil airport in the centre of the island. We managed a radio contact with them and flew in over their radio beacon at 300 feet for a low-level visual join, apparently below a stack of a dozen airliners. We had to give a cross and crusty BOAC captain a listening-to in the lift to the air traffic control tower, but we didn't care. We were young and immortal and had just beaten the odds once again.

No. 74 Squadron arrived with their Lightnings fitted with over-wing tanks. We intercepted the first three aircraft, and they were good enough to slow down and let us catch them up. When the wives arrived shortly afterwards, ours were horrified that their skirts were a good four inches further above the knee. The mini fashion was at its peak, but Carnaby Street had yet to catch up in Singapore, if it ever did. No. 64 Squadron was disbanded, and it was decided to have one last great Javelin flypast. No. 64 would lead with nine aircraft in an arrowhead with one on the box, and 60 Squadron would tuck in behind in a diamond nine formation. The double formation would make the outline of a diamond 25. The formation was shot by a station photographer at Changi going to lunch with his RAF SLR camera slung round his neck. He captured the event between two palm branches and immortalised the Javelin.

For me the Far East Air Force and carefree flying were over as I had made the decision to volunteer for the Central Flying School. I would visit in the future, and even run air-defence courses at Butterworth, but it could never be the same again.

CHAPTER TWO

THE MISSING YEARS

CENTRAL FLYING SCHOOL

The Central Flying School was one of Trenchard's three supporting pillars of the RAF, along with RAF College at Cranwell and the Apprentice Training School at Halton. In the late 1960s there were four basic flying training schools, four advanced (including the navy and army), one helicopter and numerous primary training units. Additionally, CFS Examining Wing was responsible for flying standards throughout. And it worked. At the time CFS was a form of boot camp, 'Hell-on-the-Hill', at RAF Little Rissington. Now little is left, the officers' mess boarded up and rotting, with CFS spread around the RAF.

From its foundation, CFS promoted standards of excellence. In her autobiography, Lettice Curtis recalls that the Air Transport Auxiliary[4] pilots went there to be taught asymmetric flying for light twins and all about variable-pitch propellers. There is a photographic record of pilots being trained since the 1920s, and I even found my own father, who I never knew, at RAF Upavon on the 6th War Course in the spring of 1940. Well into the Second World War qualified flying instructors (QFIs) wore elitist white flying overalls and in the 1960s being a QFI was a qualification for the Yellowjacks and the Red Arrows. Since CFS moved away from Little Rissington, which ran like a Jesuit College for pure flying, and as the RAF gradually reduced in

[4] The Air Transport Auxiliary was set up to ferry aircraft to and from operational units. Female pilots gradually moved up from simple trainers to four-engine bombers, of which Lettice herself flew around 400 with just a flight engineer.

size, CFS seems to have gradually lost its status, still with a mission to guard flying standards but through a series of CFS agencies in the various training organisations.

I had applied to be a flying instructor and actually wanted to be one. I had been positively influenced by one or two of my own instructors who had passed on their passion for flying, so here I was arriving at RAF Little Rissington. We had rented a cottage from the Northleach undertaker and were having a great time unpacking our wooden boxes which had arrived from Singapore. The course lasted for six months and was designed to reflect a course at a flying training school with three months flying the Mk 3 Jet Provost, then another three months on the Mk 4, with its larger engine. Ground school and instructional technique lasted through the first half.

Of course, we had no idea then what to expect, certainly not the monastic approach to pure flying running throughout. It gradually dawned on us that it was a privilege to be there, and once qualified as a flying instructor, you could never go back. Despite the Jet Provost itself being characterless and thus viceless, it was in fact an ideal trainer. It was hard work though. You had to know each lesson perfectly, which you were first 'taught' by your instructor. Then you flew with another course member and tried to 'teach' it to him. He of course spent half of the one-hour lesson 'teaching' you his own latest achievement. Then you 'gave back' the lesson to your instructor and he then taught you the next lesson. And so it went on. In fact, the sequence of lessons was little different from that devised by Major Smith-Barry in 1916, the founder of all flying training, actually from his frustration on the way flying was being taught in the First World War.

In the past, CFS had a few Hunters and Canberras for course students to fly. That was history, but we were encouraged to fly in the other types available. My logbook shows that I had four Varsity flights, two of which were acting as co-pilot to a Varsity course student; serious fun. I seem to have managed two Chipmunk flights while some course members were able to get flights in the CFS Gnats based down the road at RAF Kemble. Then there was the CFS aerobatic team, the Red Pelicans, named after the mascot, a pelican that lived in a Bourton-on-the-Water bird sanctuary. Since he was expected to wear a tie for special occasions, he had his own CFS bow tie as he kept tripping up on the regular model. Of course, the Cotswolds were lovely, but we never really got to explore them enough. After Singapore we were appalled by the standard of food available in pubs, when scampi or chicken in the basket were the epicurean delicacy; in hindsight quite awful. The occasional Chinese restaurant was an embarrassment.

We were a pretty ordinary course, but we were laughing at a *News of the World* article about a young lady who was making a living removing her clothes, not at all common in the far off 1960s. Her father had gone to bring her back home but was so impressed by the act that he had become her manager. The idea gradually turned into reality, and we hired her to perform at our graduation and prize-giving dinner. A large cardboard top hat was constructed to mimic the top hat awarded to the student who came bottom of the course, and this was dragged in with the girl inside. She appeared out of the hat after the said student had finished his speech and gave a brilliant performance; much to everyone's delight.

I was then posted to RAF Linton-on-Ouse to instruct on the Jet Provost.

BASIC FLYING TRAINING, LATE 1960S

I discovered the Fosse Way, then a little-used transit of the West Midlands on the way north, and arrived in the Linton officers' mess on the evening of 1 January 1968. I met up with two others from my CFS course, Ivor Gibbs and Ian MacKenzie, who have remained lifelong friends. There were just us and the barman as the station had been given an extra free day at New Year. So, we decided to investigate York in my soft-top MGB, Ian sitting sideways in the back. By this time, there was black ice on the road and we slid straight ahead at the first corner. The local farmer had thoughtfully left the gate open; the car was undamaged and we spent the rest of the night extracting it. It's amazing that we're still friends.

Although Linton was an RAF flying training school, all the students were Royal Navy, mostly midshipmen, and all destined for the Fleet. Four training flights on two Jet Provost squadrons and a further two Chipmunk flights for RN helicopter students worked in close harmony. Being a new instructor was hard work, but rewarding as our raw material became pilots. As all of them would fly from carriers we were encouraged by the navy to spend less time on those with less ability, while the RAF wanted uniform standards to apply. The navy won. Four flights a day with students at two different levels, mostly involving aerobatics, was fairly exhausting, but then there was no weekend work. There was a good social life, and Yorkshire was a wonderful place in which to be stationed.

So, after our arrivals week in the Standards Flight, I met my new flight commander, a Scotsman called Bob Fisher. "We've got just the student for your first flight. Normally the navy has no hold ups but for a small batch there has been a six-month wait for a slot at the next phase of training. So, this is all revision. Fill your boots, a bit of instrument flying, then aerobatics, then some low flying and finish off with a few circuits." My first student was totally perfect. He flew with absolute accuracy, looped through his own slipstream, pegged the height at low level and finished off with some masterclass circuits. I went back to Bob and explained that if this was a typical student then I'd better resign. Now. The other instructors on Bob's flight were clustered at the door. "We've had him for a year and he was like that on Day One. Ha ha." He was one of the world's very rare natural pilots who just knew what to do. Years later I flew a trial lesson with a policewoman at the Leicester Aero Club, who was another one, but it's that unusual.

The navy sent two general list (GL) lieutenants with every course, young officers who had completed a tour at sea, and now wanted to fly. This made it easy for us as this took care of any problems the midshipmen might have. However, they imported the navy's own 'navalese' language. "Permission to secure to my cabin", "We're taking a liberty boat into York" (a taxi), and so on. My colleague Ian MacKenzie came into the crew room after a flight with a GL lieutenant, really annoyed. He'd had to use an external battery to start his aircraft, and the GL student had turned to him with "Shore supply away, sir". The RN instructors came up with: "Next time you fly with him and see another aircraft, call it as points[5] forrad or aft the beam. He'll never work it out." On their next trip together, Ian duly saw an aircraft, worked out the number of points and called it to the GL. "His head shot round, "Got it Sir". I think he later flew Buccaneers and ended up as an admiral.

Life near York was wonderful and two military services working together was always exciting, a frozen married quarter less so. The wartime Canadians had built a skittle alley in the officers' mess roof, where many bad weather days ended. On one occasion after a week of fog, the station commander called for a walk for all instructors, over the airfield to a local pub. That was it for the rest of the day except that when we came out the sun shone and the fog had cleared. Nobody cared. We would just have to fly harder the following week to clear the backlog.

I was lucky enough to be able to invoke a Defence Council instruction, authorising fast jet QFIs like myself to be attached to a transport unit to find out about the amazing experience to be had flying heavies. That led to an attachment to RAE Boscombe Down's Transport Support Squadron and a trip in a Hastings to Edwards Air Force Base in California. It sounds awful but I loved it, flying at 140 knots and 10,000 feet, with no other aircraft nearby, via the Azores, Newfoundland and

---

5 A point turned out to be 11¼ degrees.

A demonstration of air-to-air refuelling by Sea Vixens marking the end of Royal Navy fixed-wing aircraft training.

St Louis. After days out in San Francisco and Disneyland, I was given a flight in a Cessna T-37 basic trainer, which was a bonus but really it was a twin-engine Jet Provost, again ideal for training.

The Hastings itself though was another matter. It had surprisingly well coordinated controls and was easier to fly than I expected, even landing with a tailwheel, which they let me try. The challenge was working with a crew and it seemed to the fighter pilot in me that they were quite unnecessary. So, as we approached the boundary of a flight information region (FIR), they gradually left the cockpit on various excuses. "You happy Al?" "Don't worry, I can handle it." And of course, the new FIR controller wanted a change of height, heading and then radio frequency. The engine temperatures rose and the cooling gills were a new experience. I overshot the new heading and forgot the new frequency. All five of them were standing in the doorway laughing. "OK, hot shot, so now do you know why you need a crew?" "Please just sit down and get me out of this mess." We broke down for a week at Andrews Air Force Base in Washington DC, the excuse for some brilliant sightseeing. I got back to Linton a week late, where the boss was seriously annoyed.

I had a week with the navy at RNAS Brawdy in South Wales, discussed in the next chapter, and a memorable day out on HMS *Hermes* in the Channel watching their air group working up. It was an all-day air show watching Buccaneers, Sea Vixens and Gannets launching and recovering into one of the cables[6]. In the middle of this

[6] The Fleet Air Arm Museum at RNAS Yeovilton have immortalised the 'Day Out on a Carrier', starting with a helicopter transit from RNAS Portland. A great day out.

the first navy Phantom arrived from Boscombe Down to make practice approaches, reminding me of where I really wanted to be when my instructing tour was over. It was not to happen.

The government's announcement in 1968 that Britain was to pull out of its commitments East of Suez meant little to us until the rumours started. In fact, the navy announced reductions immediately and in short order Linton started to train RAF pilots, and navy fixed-wing training was over. There had been 40 instructor candidates on my CFS course including army, navy and foreign, 40 on the previous and 40 on the next. There were just too many instructors. Then we heard that RAF Acklington in Northumberland was to close, with rumours of RAF Syerston in Nottinghamshire to follow. Then the axe fell. Forty of us between 21 and 30 months in the job were to go.

I came back from Christmas leave to be told to take my three choices of ground tour to the chief instructor, which were then totally ignored. Ian had already left on his way to Lightnings, and Ivor was grounded at Linton itself. Half a dozen of us got postings to university air squadrons on the Chipmunk, the rest got appointments within Training Command, mainly to Apprentice Training Schools. I got the Administrative Apprentice School at RAF Hereford, famous for the School

Tiger Moth and Phantom, both flown by the author.

of Catering and no airfield. So, career over, I made sure that I had a Chipmunk instructor ticket and a civil instructor's rating, said goodbye and set off, wondering if I would ever fly fighters again.

It wasn't easy. The navy Phantom was suffering from damage to its Spey engine turbines after inappropriate mating with an afterburner, and, for now, training had stopped. It all took a very long time.

A WEEK WITH THE NAVY

As I mentioned, we had no responsibility for student discipline. Led by their own commander (Air), who was assisted by a flag lieutenant, he had sole control of a Percival Sea Prince, which we used as often as we could. The instructor balance normally sat at ¾ RAF to ¼ navy. Despite being the smaller number, it was down to the latter to do their best in educating us 'crabs'[7] in all matters naval. Becoming navy savvy included days out to various carriers and the scrubbing of any student not suitable for fast jets. Sometimes, we would attend the occasional induction week at RNAS Brawdy – also known as HMS Goldcrest – in Pembrokeshire, where the students went after graduating from Linton.

So, when commander (Air) suggested it was time I spent a week down there to find out more about the navy in September 1968, I jumped at the chance. Arriving at the base, my first port of call was 759 Naval Air Squadron (NAS), which undertook advanced training using two-seat Hunter T.8s — essentially a T.7 with an arrestor hook. The RAF equivalent trainer at the time was the Folland Gnat T.1. Personally, having instructed on both tandem trainers and side-by-side, I have always preferred to be in the back for this kind of flying. It wasn't unusual for a student going solo in the Hunter T.8 to find the empty seat next to him disconcerting. Conversely the Hunter was without doubt much easier to fly than the Gnat. The course that had recently graduated from Linton had already started when I arrived, and they were loving it. I think in part this was because of the highly emancipated Wrens. At the time they did not come under the Naval Discipline Act and considered the students to be fair game. This led to several marriages.

At 759 NAS, Hunter T.8 WT722 was suffering engine issues which, luckily for me, meant a spare seat during its planned air test. Climbing away from Brawdy with the RAF exchange instructor 'Chick' Kirkham, I suspected that the cultural shock

7 Navy slang for the RAF. Crabs alludes to Crabs Fat Grey paint used in the Hong Kong dockyard and said to look like RAF blue – that's the polite version.

of flying with a 'crab' was too great for the navy instructors – but they were friendly enough. Investigating the problem probably took no more than half an hour, so the rest of the flight was mine. I was amazed at just how easy to fly the Hunter was – docile in the stall and it recovered easily. Make no mistake, I loved flying the Javelin, but it was a beast in comparison, with lots of tricks to trap the careless. It was a magnificent weapons system for its time, but it was complicated and heavier to fly. You fell in love with the Hunter at first sight; that age-old adage 'if it looks right, it'll fly right'. Chick demonstrated a simulated flame-out, and in no time had me flying what I considered respectable circuits. The end of the flight came all too soon and despite the enjoyment, WT722 had obligingly failed its air test and would need another two before it was signed off.

Around lunchtime I flew with Chick again in another spare seat while he led a three-ship of Hunters, this time in XF992. Chick let me fly, but we never told the students. This flight, for a trainee, wasn't easy. After a stream take-off, they would join onto the leader's wing while climbing in 'Vic' (an inverted V-shaped formation) very often through cloud – and then through a series of fairly mild manoeuvres and formation changes. Because of the empty right-hand seat, the student flying on the left wing frequently had the added difficulty of looking across half of the cockpit. After this we flew a tail chase, which was essentially a semi-aerobatic sequence, with the students trailing 600 yards (200 m) or so in line astern – each desperately trying to hold position. It was always fun, as well as being the students' lead into air combat training, which would be one of the main focuses with their next training unit. The flight ended in a radar to visual approach with the three aircraft in echelon, breaking into Brawdy's circuit. I tried this in an Airbus A320 some years later at Bournemouth, and it worked well apart from a hugely sceptical training captain. The passengers loved it.

The day wasn't over yet. A fellow RN instructor from Linton had been posted to 849 NAS, the navy's Fairey Gannet squadron. I had met him on arrival at Brawdy's wardroom (naval officers' mess) and he had arranged introductions. The squadron's HQ Flight, responsible for training, was here and had converted some of our students to type. Flying the AEW.3, with its air intercept radar, 849 had a flight detached to each of the aircraft carriers. I had worked with the AEW.3s while flying the Javelin in Singapore and knew that their fighter controllers were as good as any.

They also had a small number of de Havilland Sea Vampire T.22s for fighter controller training. Walking into the 'ops room' I was greeted with: "Can't fly you in a Gannet today, so how about a trip in a Vampire?" Now I suspect there was less of me 50 years ago, but I remember it was a tight squeeze. Ejection seats were only fitted in these later Vampire derivatives and they took up a lot of room in the already cramped space. During the pre-start checks, we were told to put a hand between the seats and make sure that you hadn't buckled up the other pilot's straps. It was a lovely little aeroplane, but after the first few intercept runs I started to play with the gyro gun sight, which was identical to the Javelin's and in no time I was teaching the pilot how to fly quarter attacks. The RN pilot of the Gannet target was horrified. That was my first day, and what a day! I seem to remember it ended down the road at the Ship Inn in Solva with my former Linton students, for what turned into a 'heavy' evening. What made it all the funnier was our car refused to start and we ended up being pushed back to base by the motor behind. The naval sentry waved us 'on board', and his face was a delight when we had to wait for the car behind to carry on pushing.

Tuesday started with a trip in Brawdy's search and rescue Whirlwind HAS.9 – XN311 – my first ever helicopter flight. Fitted with a manual throttle, it confirmed my total relief when I was not selected for rotary training. The afternoon was spent back with 759 NAS for another air test, this time on T.8 XL580, ending with aerobatics and circuits. In the evening it was back to basics as I took Brawdy's all-red de Havilland Tiger Moth BB694 out with another ex-Linton colleague for some aerobatics. I had flown Tiger Moths at Fairoaks in Surrey some years earlier while undertaking my RAF flying scholarship but never flew 'aeros'. However, I soon learnt the engine only restarts when you pull out of a dive.

On to Wednesday and just the one flight, back in WT722 for its second attempt to pass an air test with Chick. Once again this meant more aerobatics and circuits. I was getting the hang of it, which you do far more quickly when you don't have to remember any checks. The next day, we had to take '722 up for its third flight, which was this time successful. By now I was starting to think I mustn't take this all for granted. Despite the utter highs thus far, the most unexpected part of my sojourn was still to come. Jock Stein, another former Linton colleague, was instructing with 849 NAS. He had arranged a flight for me in a Gannet T.5, which was taking another pilot down to Exeter. In the T.5 the dual controls were only in the front and centre cockpits while the third rear cockpit faced 'aft' (backwards). This is where the passenger would sit.

Jock stopped me climbing up to the centre cockpit and pointed at the front. I had no idea at all how to strap in, let alone start the engines. Thankfully it all seemed to work, pretty much due to the somewhat sympathetic ground crew. As this was all going on, Jock chatted to me from the centre cockpit, while our passenger made rude noises at the back. Having managed to get the thing going, the [folding] wings refused to spread, and we had to do it all over again in XG883. Once finally airborne it took a little getting used to, especially as every time we turned there was a yell from behind of "RUDDER".

The Gannet T.5 was an amazing and not unpleasant aircraft to fly as we cruised at around 3,000 ft. When we eventually landed at Exeter, the passenger 'went ashore' and we took off for the return flight, which was delightfully quiet. I was almost certainly slipping in the turns though. Back at Brawdy, Jock showed me a carrier approach using the reflector sight, similar to that which a ship might carry, and we used up the fuel flying simulated deck landings. Now I had tried something like this in the Far East with the Javelin, and just remembered how the deck got smaller the closer you got. The sight really was a gift to those who could do it — especially at night. On the Friday I was exhausted, my hosts had seen enough of me, and I drove up to London in my ancient MGB. But what a week.

ON THE GROUND, 1970

I was now a flight commander at No. 3 School of Technical Training, namely RAF Hereford. There were three other pilots there at the time, who gradually got posted away. We provided a one-year training course for 15 year olds to be clerks, suppliers or cooks. We were surrounded by 50 ground branch officers, including the School of Catering, many unsympathetic to flying. It felt like Custer's last stand. The notable exception was the lovely station commander who proudly wore his World War air gunner's brevet, maybe the only one I have ever seen. He longed to talk about his experiences, and I was the only one who wanted to listen. Then, of course, he retired.

Hereford itself, city and county, turned out to be a well-kept secret, in fact another wonderful place to live. The air was pure, and the view was for 40 miles towards the Brecon mountain range. My world for now though was a barrack block with 140 apprentices, a sergeant and two RAF Regiment corporals, also a cleaner who decided to report to me daily, saluting with his left arm, and waiting at the end of the day for his work to be inspected. In theory I was the boys' commanding officer, but there was constant war with the trade instructors, who thought that they were. I guess there was mutual contempt here. I hated it, but unquestionably the boys needed me.

These were kids who had failed in their technical tests for entry and had been offered the three administrative trades I mentioned, of which the most useful was unquestionably the training to be a cook. They were generally lovely boys, but some of them had clearly come from desperate backgrounds. On their first day they went to stores and were given a mountain of kit, uniforms, sports kit, underwear, boots, cleaning kit and a holdall to carry it all. I remember one boy in floods of tears because no-one had ever given him anything. Many of them arrived with just a few worldly belongings wrapped in a brown paper parcel. In the classroom my sergeant wrote their new name and address on the blackboard, 1234567 Blank, O (a play on Blanco, a paste used to clean their webbing). A week later a dozen letters arrived from parents, addressed to Apprentice Blank O. It sounds funny but really it was tragic.

There was about a ten per cent drop out, but most of them gradually developed into fit young men with a future, and I subsequently met several of them, big strong 30 year olds who could not believe that they themselves had changed so much in appearance. That's the bit that kept you sane. There was much emphasis on physical development, including short camps in the Brecons, and a longer camp in Wales. This was called resource and initiative. Sadly, the available resource and initiative kit was old, tattered and unsuitable. I was called out one weekend by a boy whose blistered feet would go no further, then duly collected the battered Land Rover and drove into Wales to collect him. A stern local was standing with him who lectured me quire severely about the paucity of his kit. When I reported this there was little or no interest from the station staff.

I sent one of the best of them up to Training Command Headquarters to compete for a flying scholarship, which he was not awarded. However, I did get a rude letter asking us to send better candidates in future. I took a dozen of them cross-country skiing in Norway, for which the goal was a 100-kilometre two-day trek. They collapsed after a day, and I started to realise that their bodies had never been sufficiently nourished before they came to us. When the school leaving age was raised to 16, the one-year apprenticeship was cancelled. I did my best to interest them in the wider RAF and their improbable role in flight safety, including air experience flying in RAF Chipmunks at RAF Cosford. There were also a few hours for me to lecture them on wider RAF life. The head catering officer tried to get these cancelled as he thought that they were for learning checks for the air experience flying. For me the Chipmunk was a lifesaver as I also started to instruct with the Wales University Air Squadron at RAF St Athan at weekends, as well as attending a camp at RAF Abingdon.

I also started to instruct at the Herefordshire Aero Club at Shobdon, with my trusty sergeant covering for absences. I did an aerobatic air show in an Auster Aiglet and learned all about parachute dropping from a Cessna 172 and a magnificent Cessna 185. From a £3.00 per hour payment, Wendy and I took a Cessna 150 to Luxembourg for the weekend, which was a real adventure at the time, navigating with a map and stopwatch.

However, my RAF career was dead after two short tours followed by a ground job, even though, I found out later, I seemed to have done reasonably well. The Hereford experience convinced me though that I was only interested in flying. From where I stood the front line was ever receding to the point that I thought I would never get back. I described to the medical officer, a wise old Welsh civilian, images of a slippery well shaft sloping inwards. He diagnosed acute depression, except that a flying posting would surely cure it. This would stay a secret between us, and it did.

In reflection, the graduate entry did not work for all. Many of us were already married when we started flying training. The reaction was somewhere between amazement and horror, and marriage allowance was not paid until you were 25.

An air experience flight for one apprentice of No. 3 School of Technical Training.

Marching through the ranks with a flypast during the RAF Hereford apprentice passing-out parade.

Our first flat in Alnwick cost us £3-7s-6d a week (£3.40 roughly), and we could barely afford that.

Accelerated promotion though had its drawbacks. There was massive resentment amongst many of the instructors when we were quickly made flight lieutenant, while they had spent a number of years as a flying officer. In my case, after two short tours, I was through the promotion bracket before I really understood what it was. And of course, flying pay was a non-pensionable allowance, as were 40 other types of specialist pay across the three services. It was not even possible to invest some of this in a personal pension scheme until the 1970s. Eventually an offshoot of the General Duties (Flying) Branch was introduced, also around 1970, called Specialist Aircrew, for those who just wanted to fly, but even then, there might be no guarantee of a flying job.

It's just the way things were, in return for membership of one of the world's best organisations and the exhilaration of flying its aircraft. It still beat having a job.

BACK IN THE AIR, 1972

My next posting arrived eventually. I was once again assigned to fly the Lightning, which of course was for me impossible. Phantom training was still moribund while the Spey engine turbines were being sorted out. However, I had to get off the Training Command books, or I would be surely posted back to an instructing post and I kept quiet. When I left RAF Hereford, I was awarded some 30 hours refreshing on the Jet Provost at RAF Manby on the Lincolnshire coast, followed by an air-defence refresher course flying the Hunter F.6 and FGA.9 at RAF Chivenor in Devon. That was pretty exciting as I had always wanted to fly this aircraft.

The Hunter is one of the few dream aircraft ever built. I believe that the Spitfire was another one. You might think something like "I need a hard turn left", and the aircraft was already doing it. It was totally aerobatic, with a stage of manoeuvre flap with no 'G' or airspeed limit. It was a perfect air combat trainer, and at 229 OCU, RAF Chivenor, it could provide a wide range of weapons training. In the event of an engine failure, the 1-in-1 glide approach had been perfected, 1,000 feet of height required for each track mile to run, which was easy to adjust. The practice profile was simulated and practised often. Not so straightforward was where, in the two-seat Hunter T.7, the instructor would switch off the hydraulic controls and manual flying became necessary. The Hunter then had all the characteristics of a very heavy

Author flying a 45 Squadron Hunter FGA.9 during refresher flying at RAF Wittering.

aircraft, but even that came quickly with a bit of practice. I was on the short air-defence course, about 35 hours of fast-jet refresher and air combat training, ideal for the Lightning.

I let the Chivenor medical officer discover that my legs were too long for the Lightning. I tried hard to get a Phantom posting, but the OCU was still closed. While I was still dreading the outcome, one morning a visiting Harrier arrived at Chivenor and parked outside the squadron. I asked the pilot if I could go and sit in it and discovered a very comfortable and spacious cockpit. This had to be the way and in due course, I was switched to the short refresher course for ground attack. This briefly opened the door to skip bombing, what is called retard bombing (from a shallow dive), rocket attacks and air-to-ground gunnery, firing one of the Chivenor Hunter's four 30-mm Aden cannons. It was all an amazing new experience.

I was posted to 231 OCU at RAF Wittering, home of the Harrier. There would be a wait for a course slot but that was just fine. The future looked bright, and we moved into a married quarter. There was a sea survival course to attend at RAF Mountbatten (Plymouth), and a six-hour course on the Whirlwind 10 helicopter at RAF Tern Hill learning how to hover. Again, when you don't have to learn any checks or emergency procedures, rapid progress is possible. I was also given a bonus of 12 hours flying the Wittering Hunters of 45 Squadron, a unit created solely to give fast-jet pilots more flying time prior to their eventual posting to an operational OCU. I see that this was almost all general handling and instrument flying with practice approaches to just about everywhere within range. Lastly there was the usual few days of oxygen training and kit fitting at RAF North Luffenham.

The Harrier conversion was brilliantly conceived, beginning with a basic half of the course just learning how to fly this unusual aircraft, starting with two totally conventional dual flights in the T.2 trainer. Because of weight limitations we then went straight to a vertical conversion (VTOL) in the Harrier GR.1 single seater, followed by a solo conventional flight in the GR.1. In fact, we did two first solos, one vertical and one conventional. The fun started in learning the various transitions from one to the other, one dual followed by four solo. This led into the short take-off and landing configurations (STOL), followed by grass landings and take-offs, then using Wittering's very short strips amongst its taxiways and finally the Mexe Pad, a 50-metre square mat with reference markers for a vertical descent. A highlight was taking a GR.1 to RAF Newton's grass airfield, sharing the circuit with its Chipmunks, but in every case a glass-topped truck arrived with a Harrier instructor and a lifesaving radio.

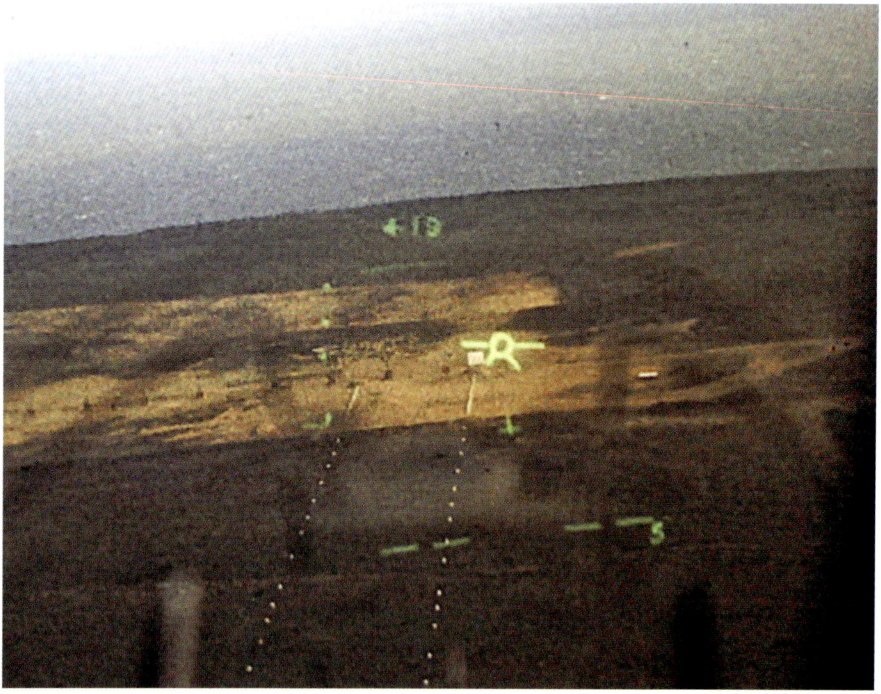
View from a Harrier gunsight during a strafe target exercise at Decimomannu.

That all took only about 15 hours of generally very short flights. The basic course concluded with night flying. The GR.1 and T.2, as the first Harrier production models, were undoubtedly underpowered and exacting calculations were needed bringing in wind and temperature before every landing and take-off. Additionally, while the two seaters and some of the GR.1s had an early model analogue inertial navigation and attack system (INAS), half the GR.1s were fitted with a P-type compass, just like a Chipmunk. The upgrades were rightly going to the squadrons, one at RAF Wittering and a further three at RAF Wildenrath in Germany. A more powerful engine in the GR.3 and T.4 would make a massive difference.

The advanced part of the Harrier course consisted of weapons training, mainly on the Wash ranges, bombing, rocketing and firing one of the two podded guns, also strike sorties around England. It soon became apparent that I had missed essential basics in ground attack, such as how to read a 1:50,000 map, essential for approaches to a target, and remedial flights were organised. The course finish came all too soon, and I was posted to 20 Squadron at RAF Wildenrath. We had bought a house in Rutland, anticipating years on the Harrier, which we now let, and drove out to Germany.

No. 20 Squadron was not a happy experience, and I was desperately underconfident. They had already shifted one squadron commander, there was a lot of tension, and I will admit having been deeply unhappy there. We went on a field exercise at Jaegergrund, closer to the Inner German border, worked the aircraft from woodland shelters, used short take-off techniques from the grass, and arrived back for a vertical landing on a Mexe Pad. The short take-off essentially was an acceleration with the aircraft nozzles pointing straight back, then rotating them to about 60 degrees down for an early lift off. This worked amazingly well and the technique followed the Harrier through to its aircraft work with the ski-jump deck designed into aircraft carriers. It was all a little unconvincing though. The fact was that a Harrier might carry two bombs 50 miles if a vertical take-off was necessary.

HARRIER NOTE

Now the US Marine Corps found that the Harrier operating from small through deck carriers was just about perfect for the marine amphibious mission. They called the same aircraft the AV-8A. However, they saw the room for improvement and after a few years McDonnell Douglas started to produce the very different AV-8B Harrier II. The cockpit was raised for better lookout, the nozzle control was beefed up for in-flight manoeuvring, better stability made vertical flight much easier and in conjunction with Rolls-Royce a far more powerful engine was fitted. The wings were bigger allowing more pylons and carriage of stores. The RAF eagerly bought more similar advanced Harriers from the GR.5 onwards, a very capable aircraft that saw commendable service in Afghanistan.

The Royal Navy, meanwhile, had adapted the basic Harrier into the Sea Harrier, or SHAR FS1, with a basic pulse radar and AIM missiles. When they went to war in the Falklands the short duration meant that the navy relied on intelligence sources to know when an Argentinian raid was airborne and times of the launch of fighters against this. They had the critical ten minutes on task and were remarkably successful in this and the basic interdiction mission with bombs. After this war, the FRS2 was developed with a Pulse Doppler radar and equipped with the AIM-7 Sparrow missile. For a while they enjoyed a full 'look down, shoot down' capability.

The end, for me, came at an armament practice camp at Decimomannu in Sardinia. I was part of a four-aircraft formation to the air-to-ground weapons range and scored a direct hit with my initial rocket. Totally exhilarated, I broke into the range circuit in the usual direction, having missed the range controller's brief that opposite circuits were in use. That was it. I was off the Harrier and back to Wildenrath to see what happened next. After a few months wait, my Phantom posting finally arrived, initially to a holding job on the Harrier simulator at Wittering, and then to an air-defence course at RAF Coningsby in Lincolnshire, via some more Hunter flying before the course started. The general view was that I had come back too far too fast from the Hereford ground tour, without adequate ground-attack preparation, and that the Phantom slot was long overdue. So it was into the car, and back to Wittering. Commuting to Coningsby looked to be inevitable.

CHAPTER THREE

THE PHANTOM

NO. 228 OCU REVISITED, 1974

No. 228 OCU was still the conversion unit for night and all-weather air defence, but it now resided at RAF Coningsby in the further reaches of Lincolnshire and was equipped with the Phantom FGR.2. FGR was the RAF's designation for a fighter employed in ground attack and reconnaissance. It had always been the plan that as the Jaguar arrived the Phantom would relinquish its attack and nuclear strike commitments and move into air defence. It was an incredibly versatile machine. McDonnell's designation was the F-4M, and it was essentially a development of the

A 29 Squadron Phantom FGR.2 flown by the author.

US Navy's F-4B, with a Pulse Doppler radar capable of detection and engagement of aircraft targets at very low level. It was never a dogfighting machine as the Americans quickly discovered in Vietnam, after which much research and training was made in high energy manoeuvring so that the Phantom might engage with aircraft that turned better. This had filtered into the RAF and the RN.

The navy had the carrier-borne version, the FG.1, or Uncle Mac's F-4K. Weapons and radar were essentially the same and a squadron (892) had been operating from HMS *Ark Royal.* The second carrier wing had been cancelled so the RAF also had the FG.1 with 43 Squadron at RAF Leuchars. You could not make it up. Then of course the Rolls-Royce Spey engines started to break up, and all Phantom conversion was stopped. I was now posted to No. 3 Air Defence (AD) Course. No. 1 AD Course had supplied crews to 43 Squadron, No. 2 AD Course to 111 Squadron in the process of converting at RAF Coningsby, and we anticipated postings for most of us to 29 Squadron. I would have dearly loved a carrier tour but was in no position to argue.

No. 228 OCU was big business. Ground school was quite formal, interspersed with several trips in the flight simulator. The navigators had to understand the radar and the navigation systems, and the pilots had to master a series of complex potential emergencies. We were put into crews, but then the Canadian exchange crew were split, and I was crewed with Gary Soule, previously an CF-101 Voodoo back seater in Canadian air defence. First though, there was the trip for a few days to RAF North Luffenham to be kitted out for the Phantom, receive anoxia retraining and to practise pressure breathing after a simulated rapid decompression if cabin pressure were to be lost at altitude.

Back at Coningsby, ground school behind us, pilots were scheduled for three dual flights before being let loose to fly with their course navigator. (By the time I got back on the staff some years later this had been changed and a flight with a staff navigator had been inserted.) Then after that the training was all about learning the missile characteristics, how to fly intercepts at all heights and speeds, some aircraft manoeuvring at a high angle and above all crew cooperation, or how to work successfully with your partner. Formation flying was the norm by day and night and there was even a spinning refresher in a Jet Provost where you recited the Phantom recovery while the instructor took the real one. We were unconvinced.

Then it was all over. Gary and I were posted to 29 Squadron as we expected, to remain at Coningsby. In fact, 29 had been a Lightning squadron and we picked up the number. We were actually a reincarnation of 6 Squadron, an attack squadron whose number had been moved on to Jaguars. The aircraft were gradually repainted as they changed role into air defence, and 29's XXX was painted on the tail. The legend was that during the First World War when 29 was formed at St Omer, the RFC depot in France, the ground crew charged with painting the Roman numerals for 29 asked, "What comes after XX, Chief?" "One X lad." However, the squadron diary told us that at the party after squadron commissioning there was a barrel of extra strong ale, with XXX carved into the wood. The squadron adopted it on the spot.

So, over the next few months the dust gradually settled on Coningsby with us and 111 Squadron in air defence and 41 Squadron in recce until they also moved on to the Jaguar. The Battle of Britain Memorial Flight had moved into the end hangar with, I think, six aircraft, and the station, which had always been a bomber base (including the B-29 Washington and the Vulcan) changed role. We were a part of 11 Group and tied closely to fighter control at RAF Neatishead in Norfolk. The locals had not spotted any difference; the early morning noise was unchanged.

NOTE

This is probably the right time to make a simple explanation of Pulse Doppler radar. Radar going right back to the original wartime Chain Home, consisted of a transmitter sending out a radio signal. If this hit something a reflection could be measured and a range derived from that. It worked well in the open air. However, pointing at the ground, everything is reflected and it becomes virtually impossible to discriminate a low-flying aircraft from everything else including waves over the sea. Pulse Doppler radar measures the Doppler shift. This simply means the difference in frequency of an aircraft coming towards you and going away. A car going past will give off a higher note until it has passed, when the frequency level drops away. So, a Pulse Doppler radar will show up an aircraft coming towards you very accurately with a bearing. Modern sophisticated systems can calculate a range from this. In practice this meant that the Javelin, for example, or a ground radar, would be unlikely to detect an aircraft at low level, whereas a Phantom flying at medium levels should be able to detect a low-level contact.

29(F) SQUADRON – ROUGH AROUND THE EDGES

No. 29 Squadron was very much an air-defence squadron, but at times it did seem like scaring the elephants away from Hyde Park. "But there aren't any elephants in Hyde Park," "Yes, effective isn't it." A part of it was the changeover where the Phantoms swapped role from attack to defence as the Lightnings were phased out and the Jaguars were phased in. It all stemmed from the TSR-2 cancellation some years previously, and the Phantom was able to plug several gaps. No. 6 Squadron had been a ground-attack squadron at Coningsby for a few years, but now the crews were posted away, and the squadron gradually morphed into 29 Squadron while the station got used to an entirely different role.

The squadron executives did not change, however. They were diehard attack experts who never quite mastered the different philosophies of air defence. In any other discipline when you go flying you know where you're going and what you're going to do. In air defence you have no idea apart from a scramble order. Accordingly, you train minutely on all the constituent parts of an air-defence mission, so that on the scramble you should have some idea of what it's about. The boss would convene a Friday afternoon meeting and go over the next week's diary which the Canadians undermined with unlimited duty-free gin and tonics. On at least one occasion he briefed the week just passed. We never minded. It was a rough but happy squadron, with aspirations to perform adequately.

The crews in fact had a depth of air-defence experience. There were those who had done North Sea air defence in the Lightning, some who had been with the navy in Sea Vixens, some from 43 Squadron (Leuchars Phantom FG.1s), people like ourselves straight from Phantom training including my own Javelin start in life, and of course the Canadian exchange crew who had flown the role in the CF-101 Voodoo; even some left over from 6 Squadron. We all had to learn the weapons systems, essentially the medium-range AIM-7 Sparrow air-to-air missile that might be fired head-on, and the short-range AIM-9G Sidewinder that engaged from the stern with expanding rods which might cut a target in half. Live missile firing took place annually at RAF Valley and gunnery at a number of seaside locations. There was some limited air combat with the Hunters from Wittering, and considerable electronic countermeasures training against the Canberra T.17s of 360 Squadron.

We quickly discovered that 29 was to be a maritime air-defence squadron. Since Coningsby was near the sea this made sense, but it did involve hours of study of

NATO as well as Eastern bloc ships and aircraft. In the event we did considerable work with ships that had fighter control, in fact the air-defence destroyers and the occasional aircraft carrier. The AEW Shackletons started to appear with the radar taken from the navy's Fairey Gannet AEW.3, which were surprisingly effective in providing air surveillance and fighter control.

We even acquired a mission against Eastern bloc Nanuchka-class corvettes, engaging with the Sparrow. To this we added the squadron's private mission against the East German and Soviet fishing fleets, maybe 40 trawlers with two factory ships sucking up North Sea fish as fast as they could. There were always a couple of intelligence-gathering boats amongst them, obvious from their aerials and lack of seagulls. These, we felt, deserved a special supersonic flypast to break a few windows, aerials and eardrums. They clearly appreciated this, judging from the pyrotechnic display as we ran in towards them. At the time the newspapers were complaining about Spanish and French theft of British fish but never the vast industrial scale of Eastern bloc fishing.

Supporting all our operations, of course, was air-to-air refuelling (AAR). The Victor K1 and K2 crews from RAF Marham were amazing flyers, who never quite received the credit due to them. They would give away their last gallon to a fighter that seemed to need it. Usually, the fighters were on the same radio frequency, but this mattered less as time went on. Mutual trust was everything, in particular when we started the longer flights. The Victors had three refuelling points, one large hose from a unit in the bomb bay, and smaller units under the wings that delivered about half as much fuel but could service two fighters at once. In the 1970s, AAR was the prerogative of air defence; later this was extended to almost everyone. The Phantom's plumbing was a probe that retracted into the aircraft when not in use, Connection was a finely balanced event gradually inserting the probe into a basket, then pushing the hose back into its pod until fuel flowed. All was controlled by a small set of traffic lights on the pod, either automatic or switched by one of the tanker navigators.

On the ground the squadron adopted the navy's 'chocolate spider' as its own drink, a fairly obnoxious mixture of spirits diluted with ice and coke and served in a pint mug. While the glass sizzled on the bar the rules would be patiently explained that this was a friendship drink which should be sipped and passed on. The wives actually liked it. However, there was always someone who thought he had to finish it off be it visiting squadrons, detachments and even a graduating Nigerian pilots' course at RAF Leeming. The squadron also produced a skiffle group complete with washboards and tea chest base, and on one occasion had to rescue a visiting wurzel (West Country) group who were dying on their feet mid-evening.

Rick Groombridge, who passed away while I was writing this book, led the skiffle group. He was the squadron QFI and he caused quite a stir when he resigned from his career path and transferred to the new specialist aircrew branch, the first we had heard of it. None of the senior officers could understand why he might want to do this but of course he just loved his flying. Indeed, he managed to stay at Coningsby until he retired after instructing on the Tornado F.3, then acting as a guide to the Battle of Britain Flight. The Coningsby area was a nice place to live in. It was quite cut off in a corner of Lincolnshire which I came to appreciate commuting there by car. There were few fences and watching the colours rotating as the seasons changed was delightful. When Rick passed on, I was reminded of a sortie I flew with him, two Phantoms against a Canberra T.17 jammer. We totally failed to spot the 100-knot jet stream blowing us out to sea. Rick landed with enough fuel for a circuit, and I landed with enough to overshoot and eject. It was a salutary lesson and simply considered to be part of the learning curve.

In the air we graduated to an intercept of Soviet aircraft at the Arctic Circle, fired missiles flying from RAF Valley and went to Malta to fire the gun. We froze in the North Sea doing dinghy drill from a Grimsby trawler and smartened up for a royal visit by the Queen. We also reinforced 43 Squadron who were holding Northern QRA at RAF Kinloss while the Leuchars runway was resurfaced. The aircraft was the carrier version, the FG.1, or F-4K, and I just remember 43's boss calling out as we walked out for our first trip, "And remember it hasn't got a battery". Folding and unfolding the wings was enthralling, so the RAF later removed the mechanism. Inevitably, someone in Germany got airborne with the wings unlocked and ejected a few seconds later.

Two weeks at RAF Valley saw us firing a select number of missiles against targets towed by radio-controlled target drones called Jindiviks. Each sortie was a choreographed ballet, with one crew designated to shoot, one spare in case the leader's radar failed, and a photo chase. Hours were spent debriefing the film to add to the RAF's knowledge of the missile. Gary and I fired a Sidewinder which flew perfectly to the target. Needless to say, the missile was fitted with a flash head but periodically a missile would be fired by the QRA aircraft to prove the entire firing system.

In a way, when the time came two years later, I was really sorry to leave. It had all been rough, tough and satisfying. The flying was occasionally difficult but always interesting. However, I was commuting every few days from Rutland and was happy to stop. RAF Coningsby, in the east of Lincolnshire was like an overseas posting without the allowances, and probably still is.

SQUADRON EXCHANGES

June 1975 – 29 Squadron/726 Squadron RDAF – The Danes
20/29 July 1976 – 29 Squadron/322 Squadron RNLAF – The Dutch

In 1975, we had hosted the Danes at Coningsby with their F-104D Starfighters. They had sent over six aircraft, half a dozen pilots and several ground crew from 726 Squadron RDAF, based at Aalborg in Jutland. They were air defence, like us, and we did some practice intercept work with them. I do remember that, as station duty officer on their arrival, I was called to an argument with HM Customs over a large quantity of Danish sausages. I had to guarantee their destruction which we carried out in the officers' mess kitchens. Those Danish pilots were more interested in seeing the UK at low level and also flying over the Faroe Islands. I did get a flight in their two-seater – RT683 – though, which was pretty unremarkable. The loop is just rather large, but the F-104 is a very pleasant aircraft to fly. I managed to return the favour, flying Lt Hoy in a Phantom. He tragically died a little later when his J79 engine suffered a creeping nozzle failure, an insidious gradual loss of power.

Our Vikings were determined that the Faroe Islanders should be treated to the sight and sound of Danish air defence, since the Faroes are an autonomous territory

No. 726 Squadron (RDAF) during a squadron exchange at RAF Coningsby.

A Danish F-104 at RAF Coningsby.

within the Kingdom of Denmark. Off they went to Lossiemouth, which was then a naval air station, for a refuel. From Lossie, they could just make the Faroes and back with external fuel tanks, flying a high-low-high profile to conserve fuel. There was then an RDAF fighter control station on the Faroes, call sign 'Pole Star', where they were particularly keen to give a show. They were back that evening, grins all round, and the low-flying and noise complaints continued long after they'd gone. Our Danes couldn't believe that a bunch of islanders could be that ungrateful. In the mean time we had sent a team to Aalborg, who clearly enjoyed themselves. They refused to discuss it. Even now.

A year later we get the news that we are exchanging with the Dutch 322 Squadron at Leeuwarden Airbase in Dutch Friesland. We had occasional contact with them over the North Sea and then two of them came for the night to sort out exchange details. One was Hennie Alberson who we'll hear more about later. He declared British Heineken to be rubbish, but Heineken Export (since discontinued) to be more like the real thing. Things were looking up already. In the July we took four Phantoms to Leeuwarden, probably six crews and enough happy ground crew. I flew in with my Canadian nav, Gary Soule.

The flying was fine. We flew a few mutual intercepts with their F-104Gs, and I had a flight in D5814 with Eric Wesselius. We met their grey parrot mascot, Polly

Grey, and we were treated nightly to downtown Leeuwarden. I took their squadron commander, Jac Browers, flying in a Phantom and we remained friends until his sad death from cancer some 15 years later. The Dutch are probably more like the Brits than any other Europeans. They like us, and they see our departure from the EU as a total tragedy, or so Rob van de Pol tells me, one of their pilots with whom I have remained friends for nearly 50 years. At the weekend, Gary flew back to Coningsby with the boss after one of our crews had successfully baled out over the North Sea. The rest of us proceeded to the seaside for a short boat trip to Terschelling, one of the Dutch Wadden islands. The night life was quite incredible, ending with their search and rescue helicopter being pushed out of its hangar to make way for the survivors sleeping on charpoys on the hangar floor.

After that it was all downhill. I flew 'a navigational training flight' to Wildenrath on the Monday to collect the duty-free for our leaving party, then Rob took two of us sailing in his beautiful Dutch barge with outboard keels, over to a boat yard in Germany, dinner of shrimp and eels, and then someone drove us back. We flew home loaded up with cheese and Boomsma Beerenburg (the local schnapps, better than Bols). No. 322 Squadron became a fixture in my service life for years to come, with many trips to the Netherlands taking in a wedding, two funerals and a divorce party. More of some of those later. Rob, now a retired KLM captain, will confirm details. British Heineken never tasted the same again.

The F-104Gs of 322 Squadron at RNLAF Leeuwarden.

BEAR D INTERCEPT, 23 AUGUST 1973

The QRA Force was rudimentary to say the least, but it worked. A room we never used, with convenient fire doors, was turned into a dormitory for four, and a telebrief was connected (on open phone line to sector operations at Neatishead). The armed aircraft, carrying eight missiles and three external fuel tanks, were parked on the corner of the apron in the open 24/7, and a Land Rover was stationed outside for the No. 2 designated pilot to drive as fast as he could to the aircraft. Readiness was ten minutes, but this was Southern QRA where nothing ever happened. Northern QRA at RAF Leuchars near St Andrews got all the trade from visiting Soviet aircraft. We were not even wearing immersion suits. However, the two aircraft were fully prepared for flight and ready to go. There was really a feeling of unreality about the whole thing though. Today it is different when the Typhoons on readiness at Coningsby might have to handle a defector or non-radio aircraft entering London airspace at any time. Nobody minded really. There was the odd practice scramble, and it was a good time to catch up on reading and television.

On this particular fine August day, Gary and I were Q1 (the first appointed QRA crew). The telephone rang and it was the sector controller at Neatishead. "Leuchars have made a bit of a mess of things this morning, and there are two more Bears coming round the North Cape. The Norwegians are with them now and we'd like to pick them up in a couple of hours' time." He gave us a scramble time and suggested that now might be a good time to don immersion suits. The unthinkable was about to happen, and we were terrified of unserviceability and having to let Q2 take the flight. As we flew north, Gary kept up a position commentary to the point where the Saxavord (Shetlands) navigational beacon (the TACAN) broke lock. He had always made the point that he was a 'fightergator' and didn't carry maps. This turned out to be no idle claim, and I had to pass my very small-scale map of the North Sea back to him.

After switching fighter control stations several times, we were working now with the Danes on the Faroe Islands, call sign Pole Star. A Victor K2 tanker materialised, which had been waiting for us, and Gary came up with the usual directions, "That's great, keep going right there. Oh, too bad, you missed", was his contribution to making contact with the basket on the end of the refuelling hose. Then he was all business as two large radar contacts appeared on the radar screen at a considerable distance, about 20 miles apart, but about 10,000 feet lower than we expected them. We confirmed "Weapons Safe", turned in behind the rearmost aircraft and identified

A Soviet air force Tupolev Tu-95 'Bear D'.

it as a Tupolev Tu-95, or Bear D, the Soviet air force maritime patrol variant. We took pictures, wrote down the door number, waved to the crew, had our pictures taken and admired their obligatory Playboy centrefold, then accelerated towards the lead aircraft. The reason for the reduced altitude became clear as one massive engine was stopped, and the crew were noticeably a little less happy. They were almost certainly in transit to Cuba from their base near Archangel, and they were determined to get there. Who could blame them?

Two more Phantoms appeared much to everyone's surprise, including Pole Star's, and we identified these as American all-white F-4Ds from the 52nd Tactical Fighter Squadron at Keflavik in Iceland, then we all flew together for the next half hour until we were told to break off. American air defence now clearly had control and would monitor their movements the rest of the way, probably handing over to Air National Guard units as the Bears reached the States. We went back to the tanker, pretty pleased with the day's work, unusual, even unknown, for Southern QRA. There was still a two-hour transit to fly back to Coningsby, and the remainder of the 24-hour QRA duty to complete. The squadron was happy; the QRA ground crew were ecstatic. For once they could see the point of what they were doing.

MALTA ARMAMENT PRACTICE CAMP, OCTOBER 1975

The Gatling SUU-23 cannon up to this point had been a mystery. It was not a part of the weapons load that our maritime air-defence role demanded. However, we were required to make a declaration of gun qualification to NATO every year, so the guns were loaded onto the aircraft centrelines, and we set off for RAF Luqa on the Mediterranean island of Malta. Pairs of Phantoms departed from Coningsby at one-hour intervals, each pair to meet a Victor K1 tanker of 57 Squadron, airborne out of RAF Marham. If a Phantom went unserviceable then an aircraft from the next pair moved up. The tanker would stay with us all the way to Malta and take care of navigation and radio as we transited French airways, where the French had cleared refuelling brackets over unpopulated areas. The refuelling went exactly as planned, then with fuel to spare we flew down the Med supersonic while the fuel lasted.

During our briefing earlier in the day, my flight leader, who had been to RAF Luqa several times in Lightnings, pointed out that the newish large RAF hangar at Luqa might cause a massive wind shear on Runway 24, if a strong wind was blowing over the hangar, and cautioned me to add 40 knots to my approach speed, which I would lose late in the final turn onto the runway. All this was carefully explained on the published airfield procedure chart. This is exactly what happened, and we

Transit to Malta with a Victor K1 for air-to-air refuelling.

landed safely, followed by our tanker about 15 minutes later. The Vulcan that arrived shortly after that was not so fortunate, but I'll come back to how this landing ended in catastrophe.

Malta was a totally delightful place to visit. There was a lot to see and do, and the Maltese bus service prior to Prime Minister Dom Mintoff had different coloured buses for each route, so that illiterate peasants, should there be any, and RAF personnel always knew which bus to take. Mintoff decided that this was insulting to his people and had the buses painted brown leading to great confusion in the RAF (and the illiterate). The sun shone, the beaches were nearby, although mostly pebble, and the wine was cheap. In all, Malta was and still is a perfect holiday destination. Fireworks were and still are endemic, the louder the better.

The gunnery was a serious matter however. The Phantom gunsights were not like the very precise reflector sights on the Hunter and the Javelin, making deflection shooting problematic, even against the large cloth targets towed by the Canberras of 100 Squadron. The aircraft radar could be locked onto the target giving accurate deflection but in practice it was almost impossible to lay the sight onto the target. In fairness, it is doubtful that the sight's designers ever envisaged this sort of usage. The squadron weapons team decided to wire lock the pilot's control switch so to make a deflection accurate at a given range, I think 500 yards, and we did start to get some hits. The Canberra crew complained that they could hear the bullets which was thought to be very amusing. Since then, of course, the problem of sighting the Phantom's gun has been quite successfully solved, of which more later. At the time it was a mystery.

Towards the end of our month in Malta, RAF Luqa received its annual tactical evaluation. The bars were closed and we became their re-enforcing fighter squadron for the next three days of essentially an air-defence exercise. The tanker crews, however, opened a bar in a spare bedroom which they ran throughout the evaluation, to everyone's relief. After three days the exercise ended and the tanker crews marched off in flying suits, followed by 29's skiffle group and many others following. At the mess entrance the procession came face to face with the funeral party returning from a service for the Vulcan crew and the Maltese casualties. It was a desperate moment, summed up by the station commander: "Every dog gets one bite, and this is yours." We bought them a chocolate spider, which they seemed to appreciate.

The Vulcan that followed us in on our first day seemingly had not added 40 knots to his approach speed, and as he hit the wind shear, he probably stalled and fell out of the sky. I was just signing in our Phantom and saw an undercarriage leg framed in the doorway, no aircraft, just the bogie. We rushed outside and saw the Vulcan climbing into the circuit with flames erupting from one wing. Our tanker pilot was walking away from his aircraft, realised what was happening, ran back to his aircraft, threw the battery switch on and transmitted on the emergency Guard frequency "Vulcan in the Luqa circuit, you are on fire, get out". The tower was paralysed, The RAF was in the process of handing over to Maltese civil air traffic, whilst the Vulcan was on an approach frequency (downstairs), and the Maltese in the visual tower (upstairs) were unable to contact the aircraft in distress.

The Vulcan pilot apparently got the message, but they were carrying two crew chiefs instead of the occasional one, and they were unable to open the escape hatch. The three rear crew and the crew chiefs were trapped. We watched helplessly as the great aircraft flew downwind to complete a visual circuit, but at the end of the leg the aircraft exploded. We saw two parachutes, the pilots having apparently been thrown clear of the aircraft, with the sickening realisation that there would be no more survivors. The aircraft crashed onto the township of Zabbar, and there were further casualties on the ground. It was an inauspicious start to the deployment. Never has an accident been so well recorded by a hundred Maltese onlookers at the runway threshold, but there is still public controversy as to what happened. I have described the accident as we saw it that day, and what I believe to have been the cause of the disaster.

29 SQUADRON SPECIAL FLYPAST, 17 SEPTEMBER 1976

On 30 June 1976, Her Majesty Queen Elizabeth II visited RAF Coningsby, accompanied by the Duke of Edinburgh. Now royal visits turn the normal working life of an RAF station upside down. Careers depend on a successful outcome, starting way above the station commander. At a more practical level they are the excuse for works services to be completed, for new carpets and curtains everywhere and for wives to buy expensive hats. The format is fairly standard, starting with an arrival to the split second (in the event by aircraft), an inspection of a station parade, a flypast, a formal lunch in the officers' mess and visits to various parts of the station in the afternoon. This one had no obvious differences. However, rejoice! No. 29 Squadron was to provide a four-aircraft flypast with a reconnaissance Phantom from our friends at 41 Squadron, flying in the 'box' position to photograph Her Majesty taking the salute.

Gary Soule, my Canadian 'fightergator' and I got the best job of all, acting as spare aircraft with a remit to 'whip in' the four aircraft as they ran in towards the saluting base. We would miss the parade and the formal lunch, but since HM would visit 29 Squadron, the wives would get to meet the Queen. The practices were hilarious. We had to get airborne at least half an hour in advance and we chose to fly daylight fighter intercepts over the North Sea, one aircraft attacking the other four. The 41 Squadron crew had never seen anything like it before and were a little disorientated above 500 feet, but they joined in and loved it. There were three practices, and at the end we let them have a try at being the single fighter. They actually achieved a simulated 'kill' and might as well have won 'Top Gun'.

It all got serious when we approached Wainfleet on the Wash, normally a bombing range, and the four-aircraft diamond closed up. Gary and I sat loose and offered tips to get the formation into an exact diamond, then broke off at low level and flew out past Boston. On the day, it all went perfectly, and HM was presented with a picture of herself which we were pretty sure would join the hundreds of others in the Buckingham Palace storerooms. No matter. In the afternoon we gathered in the squadron crew room in 'clumps of ten'. These were manageable numbers for HM and the Duke to engage with. Then disaster struck. Gary's wife Dayleen was wearing an identical dress to HM. She was pointed out anyway as a Commonwealth citizen,

Special flypast 17 September 1976.

and of course the Queen demonstrated her true style discussing fashions with her and complimenting her on the dress. Wonderful.

Very shortly afterwards, something else utterly wonderful happened. Wendy and I had been trying for some time to adopt a baby boy. We collected him and brought him home, and called him James, after my dear grandfather. The squadron were ecstatic and welcomed him. I was posted to RAF Wildenrath in the following September, but just before we left, it was annual inspection time at Coningsby from the air officer commanding. Actually, this followed the format of the royal visit very much, so everyone knew what to do. We would fly the flypast once again without the photo Phantom. That meant that Gary and I would fly in the 'box', the tail of the diamond.

Flypast timing is critical to the second. Sometimes you can cheat and let the flypast run the parade. The parade commander, in this case the station commander, receives unobtrusive signals and slows down or speeds up the parade accordingly. Alternatively, a time can be agreed and everything is geared to this, cars, VIPs and parade movements. For the royal visit the time over the saluting base was constantly being adjusted, but it worked. For the September event, we just had a fixed time. The weather was lovely, and we ran in from Wainfleet to the second, and passed over the air vice-marshal (AVM) at around 200 feet.

It didn't end there though. We stayed in tight formation and about ten minutes later, we were once again low in a tight diamond as I saw an airfield go past. "Gary did you see that?" "Sure, it was North Luffenham." They had called Wendy earlier and given her a time to be in the garden with James. As a tiny baby, he got his own flypast and welcome into the RAF. When I knew what we'd done I realised that this was my last flight on 29 Squadron, and this was the squadron's tribute to our new son. I was desperately proud of him, and nearly 50 years later I still am.

CHAPTER FOUR

RAF GERMANY

RAF WILDENRATH, 25 SEPTEMBER 1976

We knew that at some point the RAF Gütersloh Lightnings would stand down and that Phantoms would become the RAF's contribution to Central Region Air Defence. Gütersloh had been 'hardened' (that means concrete shelters for the aircraft) for two squadrons and Wildenrath had been hardened for its three Harrier squadrons. Someone, maybe in the next office, was at the same time planning to move the Harriers to Gütersloh and base the Phantoms at Wildenrath. My posting was to 19 Squadron at Wildenrath. Some air-defence crews would come from the UK, and the rest would be pilots and navigators currently in the ground-attack role at RAF Brüggen, just up the road. The aircraft would come in the main from 2 Squadron based slightly further north at RAF Laarbruch. The root cause of the mess, of course, was the previous cancellation of the TSR-2.

The Germany crews had been sent back to RAF Coningsby for a short air-defence refresher, but they were never that keen. Nobody had mentioned that it was difficult. Those of us destined for 19 Squadron met them at a meeting convened by the new squadron commander, 'Bugs' Bendell, who had been heavily involved in planning the move from the RAF Germany Headquarters at RAF Rheindahlen. It was all to be blood, sweat and tears for three months, then we would be declared operational and take over from the Lightning squadron. We were assured that the Germany crews were at an advantage as they only had to learn a new role, and they believed it. The Coningsby crews started thinking about duty-free cars. However, there would be nowhere to live until the Harrier force moved out, so we could focus on the conversion. We started thinking new cars.

I had said a rather sad goodbye to 29 Squadron, packed my MGB, said goodbye to my little family and drove to Wildenrath. I knew all the others coming from the UK, and in no time, we were at home in the wooden officers' mess, unchanged since the Sabres were based there. The next morning, we saw our new home, the old dispersal in the south-east corner of the airfield, with ten hardened concrete shelters added. The contractors had left, but their rubbish was everywhere. It was a mess. The boss declared a clean-up walk through the site over the next few days, of which the highlight was an unexplained used condom in one of the concrete shelters. A massive amount of work still needed to be done inside and out; we even laid our own barbed wire. We started to meet our ground crew, even less impressed than we were.

Well, the boss was right about the blood; that was the barbed wire. The sweat and tears came later as the aircraft started to arrive from Laarbruch, and we discovered that 2 Squadron had burnt out the near centre of the radar scopes, a function of spending their lives in the radar-mapping mode. We were working towards a fairly tight target of becoming operational in the new year, and, yes, flying in Germany was more complicated than in the UK as it was then, with civil air traffic zones, missile engagement zones, military airspace for training and airfields and always 150 miles to the east of us, the Inner German Border (IGB) and the Air Defence Identification Zone (ADIZ), for which we would be the policemen. Everything was layered in three dimensions, with military fighter control superimposed over civil air traffic control, while we would sit at five minutes' readiness with fully armed Phantoms just in case we were needed.

All this stemmed from the Bonn–Paris conventions of the early 1950s, which would determine the degree in which the emerging new German armed forces might act as the country evolved from Allied occupation. The British would station troops in the north of the country, and the Americans in the south, leading to the creation of the Second Allied Tactical Air Force (2ATAF) with a British commander, and of 4ATAF in the south under the Americans. The British had taken over a large number of German Luftwaffe bases, but constructed three new bases on the Dutch border, Wildenrath, Brüggen and Laarbruch. We undertook to guard West German airspace while the new Luftwaffe would be confined to national tasks. The arrangement ran until German reunification in 1990, and RAF Wildenrath closed its gates and runways in 1992. I digress.

Sheltering the aircraft in the new hardened shelters was a tight squeeze, and the interiors were initially awful. In time little internal cabins were constructed for the ground crew and the paperwork, also somewhere to rest. Communications were installed, and we gradually got used to turning the aircraft inside the original concrete blast pans to point away from the hangar door. An expert tractor driver would then push the aircraft back into the hangar. I don't believe that there was ever a collision. Eventually the electric winches were made to work and the aircraft would be hauled back into the hangar. Ground power electric generators sat outside the hangar making a great noise but, for an exercise, they were brought inside, deafening the crew. It just took a long time to make everything work.

The QRA force consisted of two Phantoms in the hardened shelters nearest the end of the runway, fully armed up with four AIM-7 Sparrow radar missiles, four AIM-9G Sidewinder heat seekers, and the 20-mm Gatling loaded with high explosive rounds. They were at a five-minute readiness status 24/7. Initially, damp and fairly unhygienic historic wooden shacks were provided for the two aircrew and three ground grew, but in time small bungalows were built alongside the QRA shelters. Essentially, Wildenrath was hardened for three Harrier squadrons, and Gütersloh

An armourer of 19 Squadron loading a Gatling 20-mm cannon.

Armourers of 19 Squadron loading AIM-9G Sidewinders into Phantom FGR.2 XV424.

for the two small Phantom air-defence squadrons, and of course the Gütersloh QRA facility was just about perfect. For us, it was all in the future.

However, in October 1976, the RAF Gütersloh runways had to be closed for essential work before the Harriers arrived. The 19 Squadron Lightnings were sent to Wildenrath, and arrangements were made for a parade to hand over the squadron standard formally as well as the squadron silver, to get some photographs and to have a party. I got the job of getting the pictures and was assigned a two-seat Harrier with an official RAF Germany photographer. We would fly into the local training area for 20 minutes then return and drop off the Lightning. A single-seat Harrier would be waiting and would join the formation for a repeat of the schedule.

I had been crewed with John Sabin, a Brüggen navigator, and we decided to keep it all as simple as possible. John's job was to keep us in the training area, and everything would be flown at 300 knots, climb, photographs and descent. In the event there was thick cloud on the way into the training area with tops at 12,000 feet and brilliant sunshine above. The photographer was happy and produced some remarkable results. I flew as smoothly as I have ever managed, and the second schedule with the Harrier was equally successful. (The Harrier pilot was Pete Squire, later Chief of the Air

Staff.) It was a strange experience though, flying with a Lightning on one wing and a Harrier on the other.

It was the first, and only time that I witnessed the handover of a squadron standard and it was really quite emotional. The standard was marched on to the parade of ground crew from both the old and new squadrons in white belts and gloves (in a hangar as the weather was awful). The standard bearer was escorted by two senior NCOs, bayonets fixed, who stopped facing the new colour party. The escorts made an outwards turn as if to protect the colour while it was handed over to scare off anyone intending to interfere. The RAF must have pinched the idea from the army in 1918 from a centuries old ceremony.

On then to the party in the officers' mess, when the silver was handed over. I hope our ground crew had a similar party with their ground crew, but I frankly don't remember. The Lightning squadron commander had realised that they had forgotten the beer to put in the official yard of ale, and had sent the BAC company rep back to Gütersloh to get some of the wonderful local Warsteiner. He came back with a car full which had all gone by morning. This was not the official transfer, and we were still 19 Squadron (designate), but I suspect that the informal handover would be a lot more fun. There was still a lot of work to be done.

19 SQUADRON BECOMES OPERATIONAL

Early in 1977, 19 Squadron became operational, and the Lightning squadron at Gütersloh disbanded. That's the way the RAF does it, with no particular continuity apart from the squadron number and even that is not sacred. You see this at reunions where there are cliques of ex-members from the different aircraft and eras, and the RAF is quite content to play with squadron numbers reassigned to changing aircraft, roles, and missions. At least in this case there was continuity of West German air defence. No. 92 Squadron started to form with a new handover, like 19 Squadron had done three months earlier when they took over from 92 Squadron's Lightnings. They moved into the dispersal at the other end of the airfield. The Harriers were moving and housing was gradually being made available.

I had driven back just once for the weekend to see my little son growing up, and then after two months, we were able to move into a hiring in the nearby village of Ratheim, about five miles away. A hiring is equivalent to a married quarter but is essentially a house rented by the RAF. This was a block of four houses of which the RAF had taken three. We let our own house in Rutland again and first had to see a judge in Leicester to finalise the adoption. It almost went wrong when the judge discovered that we intended to leave the country the next day, but after a heart-stopping moment, he made a new point of English Common Law and we were fine. We packed the pram top into the MGB and set off via the cross-channel hovercraft. I remember watching the baby in the mirror wriggling all the way through Belgium under the harsh motorway lighting, which was then critical for spotting the potholes.

Back at work we had actually been training pretty hard practising interceptions against each other at high speed or high level over the Belgian Ardennes, where supersonic flight was less of a problem, and we had been working up our own tactics at low level to make use of our Pulse Doppler radar with its ability to see targets against the ground. We were simulating missile attacks with the Sparrow radar-seeking missile or with the Sidewinder that would home onto a heat source. We practised identification techniques by day and night, even moving into close formation on a target with no lights, even with electronic countermeasures. This was pretty scary and was dropped from the training syllabus eventually, but night-formation flying was standard practice. Everyone had to qualify on each operational requirement.

We trained on the ground in aircraft recognition, small-arms firing, working under nuclear or chemical warfare conditions, and with our brilliant ground crew we learnt how to work out of our hardened shelters. With them we practised arming and re-arming the aircraft missiles and loading the 20-mm Gatling cannon, fitted to the aircraft centreline. We should note that in the 1970s, a concrete shelter was state of the art for protecting an aircraft against an air attack, and personal shelters were hardened in a similar fashion. That is sadly no longer the case but the shelters still serve to keep aircraft warm and dry.

We started to mount Battle Flight, the QRA force of two aircraft at five minutes readiness. We made use of the two shelters nearest to the end of Wildenrath's runway, but nothing was really ready. Over the next few years cabins gradually appeared in the shelters as miniature line offices and rest rooms, missile storage racks appeared and the very noisy ground power units were boxed in outside. Communications were the first priority as the telebrief was installed, along with a back-up battery-operated phone system. The Battle Flight doors were modified so that the station operations officer could work them remotely, for them to open together, while flashing traffic lights were installed to stop vehicle movement.

Where would we sleep? Well, to our horror, as already mentioned, wooden sheds appeared that were designed 20 years earlier for V-Bomber crews to live near their aircraft on nuclear alert. They were cramped, kitchens were primitive, cockroaches thrived and the toilets were chemical. Somewhere in the RAF there was almost certainly a maintenance unit with another 100 of them so arson wasn't even an option, and these lasted for several months. Eventually the little bungalows which were built were not unpleasant. On the most recent picture of Wildenrath that I saw, 19 Squadron's Battle Flight shelter was the only one still standing alongside its bungalow.

No. 19 Squadron was not the only unit at RAF Wildenrath. No. 60 Squadron was already in residence, flying Hunting Percival Pembrokes. The squadron number, of course, was that of my beloved Javelin squadron; so much for tradition. No. 25 Squadron occupied the north-eastern dispersal with a number of Bloodhound SAMs, still effective for a few more years. The RAF Regiment had 16 Squadron in airfield defence, initially as infantry but later equipped with the Rapier short-range SAM. The army was present with 12 Flight, helicopters supporting their commanders at RAFG, and with two troops of 21 Signals Regiment who kept the phones and radios running. All this made up a small town with married quarters, shops, a cinema, a medical centre with a number of doctors, a school, three priests and various social workers. With dependents we probably numbered around 4,000.

Looking back, I suppose that both the fighter squadron aircrew and ground crew regarded themselves as the elite, so one of 92 Squadron's artistic navigators designed a squadron patch (a cloth badge) for us that we could all wear, and another for themselves. The basic RAF badge of the 1937 design featuring our Chinese fighting

A pair of Phantoms preparing for detachment on 19 Squadron dispersal.

dolphin remained the preserve of operational aircrew in a particularly English caste system. The ground crew loved the all-ranks badge, so the aircrew quickly added a blue and white checked scarf for themselves.

Then we were ready for our first detachment. It was time for our opening session of weapons training, and this would involve taking a small detachment to RAF Valley, similar to that described for 29 Squadron. However, this did involve a number of practice sessions in the Phantom simulator at RAF Brüggen. In those far-off days electronics meant large numbers of valves, and it was fairly clear that if the simulator was moved then it might never work again. Likewise, the Harrier simulator could never be moved from Wildenrath to Gütersloh, so there were always a couple of Harrier pilots hanging round the officers' mess. We travelled fortnightly to Brüggen in the squadron Mini, mainly to practise in flight emergencies but it was invaluable for the missile-firing profiles, where every missile launch contributed to the RAF's understanding of the missiles' capabilities.

A few missiles later, after an argument with Welsh Customs as to whether we were entitled to duty-free following in the transport, we felt we were ready for almost anything. Later in the year we were sent to RAF St Mawgan (Newquay Airport these days) for a month for air-to-air gunnery qualification. We hated it. The weather was awful, we lost our Germany allowances, and 92 Squadron were going to Malta.

Inspecting the target banner to log air-to-air gunnery results, at RAF St Mawgan, Cornwall, in the late 1970s.

LIVING IN GERMANY, 1977

RAF Wildenrath was built in a hurry shortly after the Second World War. Many German ex-servicemen had been conscripted into a civilian labour corps wearing green felt battledress, working for the Allies, and available for construction work. RAF Laarbruch was even built in feet and yards by a German contractor despite being designed in metres. The rooms always felt a bit tight and the roads too narrow, but the villain has now served his term and only Ryanair go there. (They call it Weeze or Düsseldorf West). RAF Wildenrath was well built, but in a coal mining area to the west of the German Ruhr. The Dutch border was a dozen miles away, so Roermond was the easiest and nicest place for shopping or just for a day out. The Indonesian restaurants were excellent. The German Eiffel was an hour's drive to the south, leading to Aachen and then the Belgian Ardennes. Weekend excursions were easy into a part of Europe full of cultural and historical interest. Holidays were also quite straightforward and in the next three years we travelled over Europe, including Yugoslavia. I had French, Wendy had German and even the baby could babble in dialect, so language was never a problem. The trip to Berlin stands out; that was the divided Berlin with the Berlin Wall and the four-power administration still running.

You could drive to Berlin in a day with the Allied Powers (British, American, French) restricted to road corridor access via Helmsted. This was the lesser-known Checkpoint Alpha, where we entered East Germany. We needed travel permits in advance and a book of instructions at the checkpoint. Speeding would not be tolerated and there was strict guidance on what to do in case of breakdown or accident. If you met the East German Volkspolizei (VOPO for short) you had the German for something like: "I will not talk to you. Fetch me a Russian officer." The briefing did not actually say "Peasant", but this was clearly implied. However, families were encouraged to make the trip to affect a presence in the corridor.

The story goes that one young RAF officer travelled up the corridor with his wife and baby, and missed the turning into West Berlin. A VOPO Trabant was immediately on his tail as he came off the autobahn, blue light flashing. He knew what to do, and demanded to see a Russian, and after many hours a Russian officer arrived, speaking English and German and of course briefed for the event. He was totally charming and asked the young officer what the problem was. "Well, I missed the Berlin turning and was going round the flyover to go back to the junction. Now the baby is wet and screaming and my wife wants a divorce, and this idiot won't let me go." The Russian went to speak to the VOPOs and came back. "This idiot says he's been sitting here for the last nine hours waiting to show you the way back to West Berlin!"

On the day, we arrived at Checkpoint Alpha in our newish Peugeot 504, saluted the Russian sentry, had our papers snatched through a tiny grill, and then eventually presented ourselves for the same procedure at Checkpoint Bravo. Then on to the NAAFI Hotel in Kaiser Wilhelm Platz, called Edinburgh House, famous for its gastronomy (officers' side – it was run by the army). We'd been briefed that it was bad form now to refer to the square as NAAFI Platz. Berlin was divided into four sectors, the Soviet Sector, which was also designated the capital of East Germany, and the three Allied Sectors, British, American and French. The French Sector included Tegel Airport built in a hurry to service the Berlin Airlift, and also the magnificent Restaurant du Lac. The British Sector had the RAF air base at Gatow as well as the Havel Lake where, during the airlift, the Sunderlands flew in salt, while the American Sector had the regional German Templehof Airport and of course Checkpoint Charlie. The Berliners were as crazy as history records that they have always been. Nightlife thrived and the shops and hotels prospered. Jazz at the Kempinski Hotel on a Sunday lunchtime was one highlight of the trip.

As the Second World War came to a close with the German surrender, the Soviets knew exactly where the sectors would lie. They immediately constructed a war memorial near the Reichstag with two Soviet T-34 tanks. It was said that the crews' bodies were still inside. However, that gave them the right to mount a guard in what would become West Berlin, as well as insisting on taking their share of guarding Rudolf Hess in Spandau Prison, firmly in the British Sector. The Allied answer was to run military police patrols in the East and to send in Sunday bus tours. I took James to the Berlin Zoo when Wendy went on a NAAFI bus tour, conducted by an army education officer. When it was my turn, the RAF Police obliged with a Land Rover patrol. First stop was the bank to buy Ostmarks at a highly favourable exchange rate. "I thought that was illegal." "Yes sir, that is correct." I heard later that if you heard the strains of a party in the East it was probably the RAF police. However, first stop was Checkpoint Charlie. The US Army military police were immaculate in pressed fatigues, white helmet, belt, gloves and gaiters, also polite and helpful. Everyone was aware that here was a place where East Germans were dying in their bids to get to the West. This was one of the three places in Europe where we were face to face with the opposition and where in the past tanks had even faced each other. Nowadays the checkpoint is a shed manned by actors dressed as French, American or British, available for tourist pictures. It is a travesty and insulting to every person who took care of and loved Berlin.

The highlight of this trip into the East though, was probably the Soviet war memorial in Treptower Park with the massive statue of a soldier cradling a baby while holding a sword, overlooking a mass grave of probably 30,000 Soviet soldiers. We came across the Soviets again during a visit to the Four Power Air Traffic Centre. We saw the butcher's hooks in the cellar where officers had been hung with piano wire after the attempt on Hitler's life. Upstairs James toddled ahead into the ops room, so that when we got there a Soviet major had scooped him up and was giving him a conducted tour. Today this all sounds a little trite, but these were our Cold War enemy. It was the first and possibly only chance to meet them face to face. Oh well, back to work.

When we got home, we discovered that the local German police were having a police exchange with the Hartlepool force. My German neighbour was very excited by this and in the event the sight of a German patrolling with a Bobby was bizarre. No doubt it was the same in Hartlepool, having disarmed the German. The Brits had brought their police rugby team and were amazed to discover that the Germans had no idea what rugby was. The RAF obliged with RAF Wildenrath's rugby team for a demonstration match. My neighbour came back wildly enthusiastic, and now of course rugby is an established German sport. They drew the line at cricket though.

Now it has to be said that it was all too easy to live within the wire. The married quarter living arrangements made it all seem like a Little England. The padre told me that there were some wives amongst the more junior ranks who had never been outside Wildenrath's boundaries, and indeed were frightened to do so. A bus trip to the larger NAAFI at Rheindahlen was a major event. Perhaps we were lucky. Wendy was rapidly picking up German from our neighbours and I had passed my Civil Service colloquial German and French linguist exams. We were not scared to travel. We put James into the German kindergarten at the end of the road just as soon as he was old enough and in no time he was babbling baby German. (He ended up with a degree in Russian and GCSEs in five languages, and I'm sure it started here.)

However, we were looked on as a bit weird. Surely everyone wanted to live inside the wire? Even our RAF engineer neighbour's wife took her infant children into the British nursery school every day and hung around until they were ready to come home. Then she met a charming policeman (oxymoron?), and she never came back. He was devasted until her sister turned up to look after him. We loved living there. We liked the freedom to wander in and out of the German way of life (excluding the local pub on a Sunday lunchtime). We got to know the shops and especially the unbelievable cakes at the bakers. We liked taking James shopping on a sledge in the winter, and we got to know Germans. We never did meet the ones who had caused all the trouble though; they were apparently all on the Russian Front.

That said, of course, much of life did focus on the base, and not just the officers' mess. Most household shopping was from the NAAFI, the size of a small supermarket. I should explain the NAAFI. NAAFI, or Naval, Army and Air Force Institute, has served the forces faithfully for years, running shops, clubs and even mobile tea wagons, with many employees holding reserve appointments. At one point the NAAFI ran the largest fleet of road vehicles in Britain. During the Falklands War, the NAAFI manager on HMS *Antelope* made headlines when he put on his petty officer's jacket and took over an anti-aircraft gun, and on a reinforcement of a West Indian island threatened with civil strife, the mobile NAAFI was actually serving tea before the first troops arrived. The NAAFI was forever the butt of complaints but held, at the same time, in a deep affection. We shopped there. We got to know the NAAFI manager who apparently held a reserve commission as a captain. He was utterly delighted when we presented him with a flying suit which had three NAAFI trading stamps sewn on each shoulder to denote his rank. Additionally, as on most Germany stations, there were various clubs, a hairdresser, a cinema, the churches, a swimming pool and the school. Most married quarters were 'inside the wire' and it was most people's ambition to move there as soon as possible. In passing, it is worth mentioning that the Belgians also had a form of NAAFI, specialising in sausage and Ardennes pâté, as well as a magnificent selection of cheap French wines. Along with mussels and frites this had to be the star Belgian export.

Living 'outside' we were more exposed to traditions like *Altweibernacht*, a local dance night, where all the women were dressed as witches. They came and chose who they would dance with and at midnight masks were removed. While some should never have bothered, I had been chosen by the one I would have chosen myself, except that at midnight I found I had been dancing with my wife. All evening. *Karneval* was a lot more interesting, or *Fasching* in German. With Roman Catholic roots, it typically falls during the week prior to Lent, and it is usually observed outdoors with an assortment of festivities, including dancing, music, and processions. The slightly prim Rheinlanders went mad. For three days they celebrated the coronation of a carnival king, got drunk every day, and had magnificent parades which they had been preparing all year. Then on the fourth day they went back to work.

RAF Wildenrath was probably the focal point of my life in the RAF. I first went there as a university cadet in an Anson in 1962. The pilot and his passengers took me out to a forest pub called the *Fuchsbau* (Foxes' Lair) and got me horribly drunk over chicken and chips. One of the passengers was my future father-in-law. I seemed to go there again and again. When I took the family, the *Fuchsbau* was still going strong with the Germans' great sense of permanence and tradition. The base closed with little notice in 1992, and is now a set of railway test tracks, with the runway given over to open cast mining. I doubt that they miss us, but I still miss the place tremendously, and not just for the duty-free washing machine.

NOT ALWAYS A HAPPY ENDING, 27 APRIL 1977

This story has never been told before. Everyone knows about the Phantom that shot down a Jaguar, as the RAF Phantom's only 'kill', but indeed there was another one that had happened earlier. After much soul searching, I decided that it was time to set the record straight. My navigator has sadly passed but I think he would have agreed.

It was a lovely spring day all over Germany. Initially I was not planned to fly, but then a single Phantom became serviceable and ready to go. The authorising officer, who ran the day's programme, asked Monty Smith and me if we would like it. Yes, please. So, we set out a route deep into 4ATAF territory down south. The plan that evolved was a 500-ft trip down the Rhine to Nuremberg, then across towards Stuttgart, then Frankfurt and the French border back towards Wildenrath. This promised to be quite entertaining. Monty would do the work, and I would have an hour sightseeing and keeping an eye on the fuel.

So, on the southern leg of our little odyssey, and heading west, we came almost head-to-head with two American F-4Es. They were passing just to our right, so I pitched into them, aiming to get a simulated gun shot on the nearest, who was apparently the wing man. The American leader reacted strenuously, turning hard right himself in order to get behind us. So, while he was turning in my 'six o'clock', Monty kept calling out his position and what he was doing. I kept closing on the wing man. "He's converting nose up. He's well nose up. He's over the top and he's now well nose down." "Monty, he can't do that," I said, visualising what the leader was attempting. "You're right. He just crashed." I looked hard over my shoulder in time to see fire and smoke and a single parachute.

Monty made the radio call, "MAYDAY RELAY, MAYDAY RELAY, MAYDAY RELAY, Phantom just crashed at position...." and he read out the latitude and longitude, with the nearest town. Three helicopters immediately answered so we set off home somewhat chastened, and arrived half an hour later. The American wing man came on frequency, but clearly had no idea what had happened. We told him we were from Wildenrath, which he must have recorded, and we found out that he was from Hahn (which Ryanair now calls Frankfurt West).

The boss was away, so in short order we found ourselves in front of the station commander. I explained exactly what had happened and went off to write it all down. We were now grounded anyway. A few days later a senior officer from RAF Germany arrived and went through it all again. He suggested a few changes which started to alter the sense of the report, but he went off satisfied. A few days later another even more senior officer appeared and wanted more changes. It was now not even the same report, but that's what they apparently needed.

Then the American Board of Inquiry arrived, the first time any of them had ventured north of Cologne, complaining about how difficult the place was to find. It was all very formal, even though this took place in the officers' mess over coffee and biscuits, and in best uniform. A week later the Collateral Board arrived, two very forthcoming and informal pilots whose job it was to appropriate blame and make recommendations. We discovered from them that the American back-seater was tragically a steady family man and father of four. However, the pilot was a wild man with a track record of silly flying. The back-seater had in fact ejected, but he had hit a tree. Monty and I probably felt vindicated but utterly sad.

Three weeks later, on a Friday happy hour, I was taken to one side by a pilot from 60 Squadron who flew Germany's transport support. "I took the commander-in-chief to Ramstein this morning. He was met at the aircraft steps by the USAF commander." Apparently, the conversation went something like this:

USAF C-in-C: "Now what's all this about one of your boys flying one of mine into the ground?"

RAF C-in-C: "If your boys don't understand the rules, they shouldn't play. Good day to you."

We were off the hook. The boss came back and everyone was happy. Actually, we had an exercise with the Hahn Americans shortly afterwards, and we were discreetly kept out of it. Later when the station commander was leaving, I said: "Thank you, Sir for backing me up." His answer was: "You came into my office, looked me in the eye and told me the truth. You gave me no choice." As I've written elsewhere, he was a great station commander.

So, there was a second 'kill'. It was a tragic and unnecessary accident, and reminded everyone in air defence that a missile in those days had a probability of kill (PK) of maybe 0.7. The ground has a PK of one. It took me a year before I could press a shot on a training interception.

GÜTERSLOH BATTLE FLIGHT, 21–23 NOVEMBER 1977

The origins of Battle Flight were in the 1950s when the Allied Occupation of West Germany finished and the new *Bundeswehr* was established in 1955. The RAF and the USAF retained responsibility for the peacetime air policing of West German airspace. The two hardened shelters nearest the eastern end of the Wildenrath runway were each assigned to a fully armed Phantom as previously described, also a rather good SLR camera secured in an unofficial special bracket. The shelters were modified so that the massive metal doors opened together, lights flashed to stop vehicles and a strident hooter sounded. A pilot, a navigator and three ground crew shared an adjacent bungalow for 24-hour duty periods at a five-minute readiness, which generally meant sleeping with boots on. Meals were delivered. Dutch TV, with all the 1970s comedies, was obligatory.

One shelter nearest to the runway belonged to 19 Squadron, and the other to 92 Squadron. It was a strange relationship. Air-defence doctrine had long since moved to working as a pair, but the Wildenrath establishment of Phantoms was embarrassingly small, with around 25 in total over two squadrons, while our NATO partners fielded 36 fighters to a fighter wing and the USAFE fighter wing 72. So instead of scrambling a pair of fighters the RAF had arranged to send just one. And, of course, if the aircraft became unserviceable it took a long time to prepare another. The two Battle Flight aircraft therefore tended to work in isolation, and, with a cuckoo in one of our hardened nests, usually a couple of our aircraft stayed outside in ancient blast pens. However, if a squadron was away the other had to double up, and this was the case when it was decided to test Battle Flight's forward deployment to RAF Gütersloh, about 100 miles to the east nearer to the IGB. Our Lightning predecessors had been based there, and a soft-skinned Battle Flight pair of purpose-built hangars had served them well. Currently the resident Harrier squadron used it as a car park.

I was 19 Squadron's Battle Flight officer, which sounds grand, but in practice it meant that I had to produce an ever-contested monthly roster and the RAF paid for me to have a phone at home. I was told 'in secret' that we would be deploying Battle Flight to Gütersloh at short notice (enough for air and ground crews to come in with a packed bag), but for our hosts it would be a complete surprise, announced when the aircraft were on approach to land there. Naturally I rostered myself, and for once we scrambled as a pair for what was known as a border patrol; showing the flag at the border in effect, and landing at Gütersloh. Arrival was actually quite funny. We sat just outside the old Lightning facility, engines running, while there was a mad scramble to move enough cars to let us through. The cross-servicing flight helped us to set the aircraft up at five minutes readiness while our own ground crew arrived by road with a third aircrew. It all went rather well. We did a couple of border patrols the next day and flew home the day after. The second evening was, for me, the one you don't forget.

It was my turn to stay in the officers' mess with Noddy Halsall, my established nav. We had Göring's famous falling beam demonstrated a few times in one of the towers, then someone asked who would like to visit the German Paderborn Flying Club. It was a thoroughly pleasant evening and I ended up talking to the inevitable Second World War veteran at the corner of the bar. He was quite amazing and he had flown all the fighters, the Me 262 jet and even the Me 163 rocket fighter. He was very interested in what we were doing until it was time to go. "I'm sorry," I said, "I didn't catch your name". "Oh, Galland," he replied, "Adolph". "I have thoroughly enjoyed our evening talking together."

I checked in a library book when we got back to Wildenrath, and for sure it was him. What a gentleman. What a man.

CHAPTER FIVE

TRAINING FOR WAR 1978

YOU FIGHT LIKE YOU TRAIN – DON'T YOU?

This simple aphorism gradually became the unofficial basis of NATO flying. That started with the equipment issued, and the various procurements by the British government have not been a great success story, and all too often what might be best can be overridden by politics. Even the Phantom turned out to be the heaviest and slowest ever built with Rolls-Royce Spey airliner engines, whose turbines initially disintegrated from the effect of the added afterburner. Many mistakes were made with its equipment, such as lack of radar warning which would have come as standard with the aircraft, and lack of electronic countermeasures. As the UK intended to fly the Phantom from two aircraft carriers (reduced to one), we bought and modified the US Navy's F-4B, with its Pulse Doppler radar. We have discussed the missiles and the cannon elsewhere, but we discovered through an attempted missile cross-servicing with the USAF, that the USAF AIM-9 missiles would not connect to US Navy missile rails. Many of the Phantom's connections were non-standard and would not fit NATO equipment, and we had wheel brakes designed for aircraft carrier parking rather than stopping after landing.

All of our training therefore made use of the aircraft's strong points, like a two-man crew and an excellent radar (when it worked), and sought to minimise the disadvantages. We have discussed the layered training and specific parts of the operational requirement, and the fact that on a 'scramble' order you never quite knew what to expect. Sometimes, when the shelter doors opened, it was even a surprise that it was raining or indeed night time. So, we had to be ready for anything and then exercise as realistically as possible given the airspace and eternal noise problems, which precluded the use of afterburner below 3,000 feet. That stopped you turning properly. In fact, to police the noise constraints, the German Luftwaffe procured a radar/optical system called *Fledermaus* (Bat) that measured height and speed as well as taking film. The first offender fortunately was a German recce pilot in a McDonnell Douglas RF-4E Phantom from Leck, who turned straight into the radar and dived into a low attack. What a star! The Germans made it clear that there would be no action this time, but heaven help the next offender.

The station would therefore go onto a warlike footing every few weeks, sometimes just RAF Wildenrath, which was called a Minival. Everyone on the station was involved although it was bizarre to see the shops and school open as usual while we went into NBC (nuclear, biological and chemical) gear wearing gas masks and toting our 9-mm Browning automatics. These were later changed to the more Bond-like Smith & Wesson. (The first pair who went to the range to qualify turned up in dinner jackets, much to the disgust of the RAF Regiment host who we thoroughly disliked.) Apparently, these lighter guns did not crack ribs should you have to eject from the aircraft. From time to time the whole of RAF Germany might 'go to war', involving all four flying bases. My next navigator, my lifelong friend Tony Parker, put paid to the RAF Regiment instructor during gas training. The exercise was called 'buddy change' where inside a gas tent you changed gas mask filters with someone else. The Rock Ape paired himself with Tony, and the last we heard was "You bastard, Sir" as the Rock threw himself outside the tent with lungs full of gas. We didn't like him anyway.

Then beyond that the entire ATAF might launch an exercise, sometimes both 2ATAF and 4ATAF, with the entire ground environment (the missiles, the radars and even the army). These exercises were massively entertaining, when just about any aircraft you saw might be a target ready for an attack, although the rules were quite strict to prevent low-level dog fights. Our problem was that once again our air lords had not thought through the issue of taking the RAF Phantom from its ground-attack and strike role into air defence. The standard camera was simply clipped onto the gun sight where it covered the radar. Even then the pilot had to set the exposure manually, guessing the light conditions, and possibly in a tight turn while he did so. Eventually a rather complex camera was introduced some years later, but nowhere near as effective as the one we could have bought with the aircraft. I should have explained. In peacetime no actual missiles or bullets were intended. Gun camera film was essential to find out whether weapons were simulated in their 'kill' envelopes, but more often than not we ended up with unusable film.

Once a year every base was evaluated by the headquarters above the ATAFs – the Allied Air Forces Central Europe (AAFCE) – by a permanent team of experts drawn from all the air forces and all the operational disciplines. This tactical evaluation was simply known as 'Taceval'. The team took no prisoners and reported as they saw it. Careers could be made or broken on the results. In air defence there had to be an element of surprise, so the first the base knew was the team arriving with "Hello, we're at war". They would already have sneaked in spies to watch how the Battle Flight reacted, always with a scramble for a border patrol. Then they would evaluate the war generation of each unit, with the squadrons calling in aircrew and ground crew and gradually producing armed serviceable aircraft. There were strict targets that had to be met as the station went to war.

Occasionally the exercise went straight on into the rest of a five-day war, but not always. Sometimes the team came back on an agreed date and watched how the base coped. There was constant action, with crews flying maybe four times day or night, with team members occasionally flying along as chase, to check that we were doing what we said we were doing. The Achilles heel was always the transition into the NBC phase of the 'war', where no base had ever achieved the top score (one, two, three or four). At the time nobody had genuine protective equipment, but we did our best with what we had. On my last Wildenrath Taceval, we scored a four for the NBC phase, known as 'survive to operate'.

John Mitchell had been the best station commander ever, and this was the station's personal tribute to him. One of the team members told me later that he and another had been quietly watching 19 Squadron in the small hours of the morning, as an air raid was called. "Attack, attack, attack." One of our ground crew was arriving for a shift change and despite his not knowing that anyone was watching, he dived into a ditch, yelled out, "Gas, gas, gas" and donned his respirator. The team was convinced. "These boys deserve to survive on what they've got." We never did find out who this star player was. In fact, any of us would have done the same.

Even before I had taken part in a Taceval, the boss came into a squadron Friday afternoon meeting and asked who would like to be a guest member of a Taceval team. Two of us jumped at the chance, so he threw a cigarette packet in the air with "heads or tails?" It was Player's Navy Cut, so at least it had a sailor's head. Well, I won the toss, and really it changed things for the rest of my time in the RAF and afterwards. My first Taceval would be, strangely, to my friends at Leeuwarden with their F-104G

Flying the F-15 at Bitburg AFB on Taceval.

Starfighters. As I knew them when I walked in prior to the start they all burst out laughing. It was not such a great secret after all.

However, I learned a vast amount about how another wing operated in the same conditions as ourselves. I flew twice with Rob van de Pol in a F-104 two-seater, on one occasion as a target through the Dutch islands. I brought back a number of good ideas that we might use at Wildenrath and thought that was the end of that adventure. However, I must have done reasonably well as they asked for me again, and over the next few years I took part in the Taceval teams evaluating the Germans at Neuburg in Bavaria with their F-4F Phantoms, the Americans at Bitburg in the Eiffel with their newly arrived F-15A and F-15B Eagles, the Germans again at Wittmund on the north coast, and the Americans at Soesterberg near Amsterdam. The Americans and Germans both arranged air-to-air live gunnery over the North Sea, the USAF using air-to-air refuelling to get there. I flew 'chase' with all of these and learned that the boom operators in the Mildenhall KC-135 Stratotankers were all identifiable by their farmer's flat caps, their own bit of elitism. Having the refuelling boom smash into your aircraft was just a little different from the fine and delicate art of inserting your refuelling probe into a basket run out from a Victor tanker.

All this pushed me progressively into a love of ops management where I could see very clearly what we were doing right or otherwise, and where our equipment was letting us down. I probably hoped that the reports generated might lead to improvements, but I doubt that they did. It could not all be excitement though. One morning I was on my way into work expecting to hold Battle Flight for the next 24 hours. The boss was standing outside the squadron: "Get changed as quick as you can, and I'll be up to brief you shortly." It went something like this, that the previous evening one of the *Rote Armee Faktion (*Red Army Faction) was shot in jail. The rumour was that the German police did it, and that the terrorists would hijack a civil airliner and crash it into the Parliament buildings in Bonn. The German chancellor called the British prime minister, Mrs Thatcher, in the night to ask if she would honour the Bonn–Paris convention and stop them, by shooting the airliner down if necessary. Despite this being a national event, his own German quick reaction flights were on the northern and southern borders, while the RAF were very close to Bonn. Mrs T immediately agreed, and got the commander-in-chief out of bed in the early hours of the morning. He in turn roused our station commander, he roused the boss and now the boss was briefing me.

You can imagine that this was a conversation stopper. We sat all morning in silence while the ground crew tiptoed around us and brought us tea. By lunchtime though, nothing had happened, and then lunch arrived. My nav looked up and asked me: "Which weapon do you think we should use?" I had been thinking the same thing myself.

GERMAN NEIGHBOURS

It was time to make some friends. Our German neighbours generally knew little more about us than the noise we made, and many of the British found trips into Roermond easier than visits to the German townships. RAF Wildenrath's station commander, John Mitchell, decreed that each of the three flying squadrons would 'adopt' one of the local towns, the nearest physically in fact. No. 60 Squadron drew Wassenberg, the closest, really just a large village, 92 Squadron got Heinsberg, the county town, and 19 Squadron got Erkelenz, just a few miles away to the south-east.

Erkelenz was a pleasant enough place, with at least 1,000 years of history, but it had been through turbulent times, even becoming at one time a part of the Spanish Netherlands. Towards the end of the Second World War, it found itself positioned on the division line between the American and British armies. It became pivotal in the German defence, and received very heavy damage from aerial bombardment. The population left in droves, at its low ebb reducing to just 25. Afterwards, in addition to its returning population, the town received large numbers of refugees from the Eastern German territories. In many ways it was rebuilt and had to start again as a new town. It was occupied in turn by the Americans and then the British, who managed to establish reasonably good relations.

I am unsure how our first contact was made, but I well remember the cocktail party where we hosted the town's great and good. The town's long-term mayor, Willi Stein, seized on the squadron drink, the 'Blue Dolphin', pointing out to everyone that the colours were those of Erkelenz, and he renamed the concoction of blue Bols floating on clear Steinhäger (a German gin), '*der Blauer Delphin*'. After a quick manufacturing session, it became the official town drink and friendship was sealed. A number of reciprocal invitations followed, including the *Karneval Prinzenfrühstück* (the Carnival Princes' Breakfast) to be held just before Lent. The boss, Norman Browne and I went, and we took the blue and white dolphin, more of which later. This would be the last day of parties, where the *Karneval Prinz* would be crowned. I guess the event was a bit like British Lions, except that it was an alcoholic breakfast before the parade. The mayor was cradling a pint of '*Blauer Delphin*'. The German women unsurprisingly loved it.

Our chequered dolphin was a great success, and Norman, Dolly (as we now called the dolphin – more about her later) and I were invited to another office party at the top of a tower block. The boss went home to bed. The party was in full swing with office girls in fishnets, boots, bodices and tricorn hats marching up and down, all wanting to kiss the dolphin. Someone looked out of the window and saw that the parade had started, missing the girls who should have been leading it ahead of the town band with the glockenspiel. We all rushed six floors down to the street. Norman and I were fast losing spatial awareness and gratefully spotted the squadron float. We had taken a few liberties with local history and built a Roman encampment on the lorry, with a catapult that fired sweets into the crowd. After all, didn't Caesar invade England with the Belgae cavalry? Norman and I just sat beaming at the crowds.

Then onto the annual Battle of Britain cocktail party, held in the officers' mess in September. It was called the autumn cocktail party so as not to cause any offence. The *Stadtdirektor*, Berthold Jansen, was there with Willi Stein, a mixture of executive town clerk and enforcer. He was the brains. "Herr Munro, why do we always hold this cocktail party in September?" he asked innocently enough. "You know perfectly well why. Anyway, I always wanted to ask you why you're so helpful and friendly to the Brits." "That's easy," he said. "When I was sixteen, and the British Army was crossing into Germany I was forced into the *Volkssturm*, given a uniform far too big for me with blood and bullet holes, handed a rifle and told to shoot the first British soldier who crossed the bridge." "What happened?" "Well, I did, and the British took my rifle, smacked my bottom, sent me home and told me not to do it again. No other nation in the world would have done that, so now you have my total respect and loyalty." Wow! Who knew?

Shortly afterwards a new *autobahn* spur was to be opened connecting Erkelenz to the national network. The boss agreed to provide a flypast, himself leading, with myself on the right and Jack Hamill on the left. We were air defence though, not used to times on target, and the truth is that we messed it up. We were early, so the boss slowed down. Jack and I each realised that the noses of our Phantoms were gradually getting higher and then the rudder pedals started to shake. This was the aircraft warning that it was about to stall. Jack and I eased out and increased speed, and we never got back together with the boss. The picture in the paper was of three Phantoms in a gaggle flying over the tape-cutting ceremony, and the caption read: "The British Royal Air Force flew past in tactical formation." They never found out the truth!

Erkelenz was a nice town with good people. They liked us and looked after us.

NEW YEAR'S DAY SCRAMBLE, 1978

Someone had thought that it might be a nice idea to scramble off Battle Flight at midnight on New Year's Eve, then fly round North Germany wishing all our colleagues in Fighter Control a happy new year from RAF Air Defence. That of course would include a border patrol along the IGB. I'd got the job, so missing the New Year's party would be my reward for running Battle Flight. We decide to go anti-clockwise. It had to be better than seeing the New Year in watching Dutch television over a mug of tea. The boss had liked the idea.

My partner for the gig this time is Mike Stephenson, a really nice man and recently engaged, who was tragically killed in an air accident after he returned to the UK. This time there is no rush though. We saunter out at about 20 minutes to midnight on 31 December 1977. It has been a brilliant year, introducing the Phantom to Germany and taking our place in the Cold War. Much of it is still a novelty. The blast doors are open, the ground power is running, and it makes a real change not having to rush. At five minutes to midnight, we have the engines running, the inertial navigation in navigate, and the ground crew are happy that the aircraft is ready to go. The operations officer, from his desk in the Command Centre, has made up a suitable scramble order so we wish him and all at Sector a happy new year a few minutes ahead of time. We taxi out to the runway, and are cleared to line up and take off.

Mike counts down to midnight. "Five, four, three, two, one, GO," and I release the brakes and select full afterburner. I'm hoping that the locals appreciate the noise. I wish the tower controller a happy new year and then fly a fast lowish circuit of the airfield. I roll out so that the Malcolm Club, the airmen's mess, the sergeants' mess and the officers' mess are pretty well lined up. At about 300 feet in full afterburner, we fly over the lot. Two squadron members are standing just outside the French doors and afterwards they seem to be the only ones who noticed. German noise at midnight on new year is incredible. Years later I'm working with an ex-12 Flight Army pilot who lived in the village apartments, who mentioned that some idiot had overflown the flats and woken up the kids. I couldn't tell him.

So over to Departure, happy new year again, and then once more with the Luftwaffe air traffic controllers at Clutch Radar (part of Düsseldorf ATC). "A Happy New Year from RAF Air Defence." By this time, we're level at 10,000 feet, and we can see fireworks exploding in every direction. We ask if we can do a fly-by at RAF Gütersloh. The answer comes back, "Don't you know we have a noise problem?" Then it's a short climb and into the ADIZ along the IGB. We talk to each of the Luftwaffe fighter control centres in turn, all with the same happy message. They seem pleased to hear from us, call signs 'Backwash', 'Loneship', and 'Silver Cork' as we fly north.

In the middle of this Mike says: "SAM10 lock three o'clock. His radar-warning receiver is alight, but the grateful government has not seen fit to give me the standard fit repeater scope in the front cockpit. It's a new missile deployed with the Soviet Forces in East Germany. I transmit: "And a very happy new year from RAF Air Defence to all our listeners on the other side." The lock vanishes a few minutes later. Now we're north near Bremen and we turn west out of the ADIZ. Next for new year greetings is 'Round Up', in German Friesland, then the Dutch at Nieuw-Milligen, call sign 'Bandbox'. We're nearly home, with two to go. We call the fighter control next to our Sector Operations Centre at Uedem, call sign 'Crabtree', then the Belgians at Glons call sign 'Efflux'. It's after one o'clock on New Year's morning.

We shut down in front of our shelter and our ground crew push the aircraft in with the tractor, to be got ready to go again at five minutes readiness, and we once again prepare the cockpits. Finally, we get a cup of tea and celebrate our own new year 1978 with our three engineers. Was it totally pointless? We didn't think so. Hundreds of service men and women were on duty at that very moment doing their bit to keep the world safe while everyone else was having a party. We generated massive goodwill that night, that ran on into the following year, and for a few precious moments, we brought our colleagues together; even the ones on the other side of the border.

WINTER SURVIVAL TRAINING

I had been sent on the RAF Germany (RAFG) two-week winter survival training. This all took place in the rather lovely old Hotel Zur Post in Bad Kohlgrub, not far from Oberammergau. The RAF took over the cheapest rooms and the cellar was kitted out as a survival school. The arrangement had been running for years, and, it seemed, everyone was a winner, well almost everyone. For the first week you skied. However, no lifts were allowed, and it was supposed to get you a little fitter. There was classroom work in the morning before the snow and after dinner to keep you away from the bar. In the second week you spent a few nights living in the snow then, if you're unlucky, a night with the interrogators.

I met one of the squadron navs, Pete Smith, at the RAFG Headquarters at Rheindahlen on a Sunday morning, and we said goodbye to the highly amused wives and children. They had seen the transport to Bavaria, a small bus, almost certainly just one previous owner, namely the Wehrmacht, and they wandered off to have a coffee. The other candidates were from many of the other RAFG squadrons, and we got to know each other as we rattled our way into southern Germany. The snow thickened as we went south.

Now I have to admit that apart from having to walk up the mountain, the skiing was fun and the classroom sessions were absorbing. Evenings after work were spent in the hotel bar after a great dinner. The staff told us that on one distant previous course, one participant was missing after *Rosenmontag* (a part of Lent). With gritted teeth they took the Land Rover into Oberammergau and found the missing pilot leading the town band into the next pub. He was gratefully extracted and put to bed.

The RAF principles of survival are invariably protection, location, water and food. You can last a long time with no food but you can die of exposure overnight if unprotected. So, we learnt how to make best use of the equipment packed into an aircraft ejection seat. We learnt how to make shelters out of parachutes, or even the life raft. We learnt signalling to rescuers and how to light fires. We'd never forget that the moss grows on the north side of a tree. In passing we heard that a sharp stick is invaluable for pegging down a parachute, so the village ironmonger did a roaring trade in six-inch nails. The instructors also kept talking about a 'go-pack', a cigar tin with useful items like water purifiers, Bovril, rabbit snares and a fishing line, and we should always apparently fly with one. More ominously we started to learn how to evade hostile troops should we be shot down, and how to behave as prisoners. It was naturally assumed that the opposition was non-violent and didn't use drugs. All too quickly though, it was time to start the field phase.

The bus appeared again and we were off into the forest. Pete and I were naturally paired up and then the pairs were dropped from the bus at intervals. We had to walk into a forest site, where we would survive for the next three nights. We were wearing typical winter flying gear and we had all made packs to carry the seat survival gear and a life raft. In those far-off non-PC days many of us smoked, in particular the small cigars that the NAAFI sold by the gross. How else could you make a go-pack? Those were allowed, alcohol was banned and they probably already knew about the six-inch nails.

For night one, we were on our own but we could see everyone else. Everything was wet and only a few of us got a fire going. It was a rotten night. The next day, Pete and I stumbled on through the fairly deep snow, set up our parachute shelters, and each decided to sleep in the life raft, not easy when it's freezing outside and you're over six feet tall. We got a nice fire going with standing dead wood, and decided to take turns being mum and dad. Mum's job was to tend the fire and keep feeding in a dead pine tree from each side of the fire, as well as keeping a non-stop supply of soup or Bovril for dad when he came back with another dead tree. Dad's job was to make sure we didn't run out of dead trees. The trick was to find a tree that had died but was still vertical. Once they have fallen, they quickly rot and are useless.

After a slightly better night, I was mum, and we had a visiting air marshal, good breakfast, beaming face, and fully briefed. "Don't get up!" I'm not sure I could have done after a night like that. "Ah, I see you have a go-pack?" "Yes, Sir." He had had the briefing. The tin is bright orange so he had done well. "And what is in your go-pack?" "Nineteen cigars, Sir. I just smoked one." He was shocked. "Do you fly with a tin of cigars?" "I certainly do Sir. More useful than a fishing line." I got the air marshal's dead eye as I was clearly a moron and he went off to find someone who fished and understood air marshal talk.

That was it for day one, apart from learning about different types of shelter. On day two we were introduced to four massive live white rabbits. Our instructor – a pretty horrible member of the RAF Physical Education Branch, that we called 'muscle mechanics' – explained that each rabbit had a different colour ribbon representing each pair and the aim was for us to catch and kill our rabbit. He thought this was hilarious. We thought roast rabbit for lunch. I think at some point we had to break camp and set up again after a short trek, all to get us pretty tired for the evasion phase. We had to walk out through 'enemy' territory. The bus re-appeared and again we were dropped off in pairs at intervals. Each pair had a map and we had a 'safe' objective a few miles away on the other side of the exercise area, The night was crystal clear and the snow was crystal crunchy. The 'enemy' was a detachment of German army ski troops. No fighting; if one touched you, you had been had. Of course, one or two of the smart escapees waited until the bus had gone, got in a pre-ordered taxi, and went to the pub, appearing at the objective a few hours later. Pete and I just marched in a straight line and hoped for the best.

Then we came to a forest road. Crunch, crunch, crunch. "Let's tiptoe over the road as quietly as we can." What a daft idea, especially when a ghostly shadow leapt out of the ditch. "HALT." We outran him for about ten yards, then he marched us off to his company headquarters in a forest barn. We met his company commander, a German army major with ambitions in amateur dramatics. "Good evening. For you the war is over. Would you like a coffee? Chocolate? It is English." He had seen the movie. Just as we started to relax, there's a shush! And we heard crunchy footsteps outside. "This looks like a good place to hang out for a couple of hours." In through the door came a pair of Jaguar pilots. "Good evening. For you the war is over." Then after he had caught a few more it was, "Now sadly it is time to introduce you to a colleague who is not so nice."

And very soon we were stripped, bag over the head, damp overalls, white noise and squatted on the point of the backside, hands behind the neck. Luckily waterboarding has not yet been invented yet. Then it was off to the first interrogator. He was the idiot, Mr Clown. He dropped things on the floor, he spelt everything wrong and spilt his coffee. "I'm sorry Sir, I cannot answer that question." He had an apprentice though, a young army officer, a Rupert, who got bored. "Twenty press-ups," and the spell was broken. In the course of a long night, I met Mr Organiser who wanted me to help with prisoner welfare and then Mr Nasty. The fourth time the blindfold came off there before me sat a proper naval commander who said, "Well done, it's all over." "I'm sorry sir I cannot answer that question." They had to get the doctor, who was neutral, to persuade me that it really was over.

Back in the Zur Post, we saw that we had black numbers painted on our hands and foreheads. Granny came up and asked what we were having for breakfast. As one we said "BEER". She said that was disgusting but the landlord said it was fine. In the evening, we met our interrogators. It seemed that it was a part-time job; in fact, Mr

Organiser was a mild-mannered bank manager. They were clever though. The French air force pilot who attended forgot how to speak English, so they just continued in French. Mr Clown said: "You know your weak point now. I nearly had you there, any ruse to get you talking. If you'd tried to help, I would have got you, and I think I nearly did, if Rupert hadn't interfered. Please, always beware the clown."

I still have problems working out who the clever people are, pretending to be clowns, and who the clowns are, pretending to be clever.

SUPERSONIC DOLPHIN

We had been deployed to RAF St Mawgan again, by then a Maritime Support Nimrod MR2 base. The runway is massive and the delivery pilot from the maintenance unit at RAF St Athan, claimed to have landed a Beaver across its 300-yard width, when the wind was too strong across the main runway. We were not immune to the charms of Cornwall, had some sympathy for their concepts of Cornish nationalism but, well, it was boring. Beer was expensive, we had no cars and the grateful government removed our overseas allowances while we were back in the UK. There are only so many pasties that you can eat. The summer weather that year was pretty awful, and our sister squadron, 92 Squadron, had been sent to Cyprus instead. The year before it had been the same, but we travelled in hope. This time we knew what to expect. Rain.

The aim of this deployment was what's called an armament practice camp (APC). We were joined by three Canberras from 100 Squadron, equipped for towing the target flags favoured by the RAF, and in this case air controllers were waiting at a large area of sky marked off as a firing range just off Hartland Point. The idea was for crews to fire the underslung Gatling cannons at the towed flags with ball rounds dipped in various colours of paint. In that way hits for individual aircraft could be counted after the flag had been brought back and dropped. Typically, four or five fighters would fire at one flag, and a percentage score could be calculated. The aim was to qualify against a NATO minimum, the score being worked out as a percentage of rounds fired. The fire rate for this kind of practice shooting was reduced from the usual 6,000 rounds per minute to a modest 4,000. One very short blip on the stick top trigger might shoot off seven or eight rounds. However, while the gun sight was slewed to the radar, infinite skill was required to bring the rounds to bear. We spent the first four days talking about it, waiting for the clouds to lift.

On the Friday, the sun came out at lunchtime. I was running the desk and with the two operations clerks, the weapons instructors and the ground crew, especially the armourers. We decided to see if we could put up 20 flights in two waves in the course of the afternoon. We had ten Phantoms and the three Canberra tugs. Hartland agreed to split the airspace in two so that we could work two flags simultaneously and amazingly nobody went to the wrong flag.

Then the fun started. We had to programme crews so that everyone had time to brief, fly safely and then have a weapons instructor review their gunsight film before they flew again. Canberra ops had to match their flag times to ours and one Canberra crew would have to fly twice. The armourers had to keep the guns topped up and make sure that aircraft for each flag fired different colours, by dipping the bullets as required. And our dear wonderful ground crew had to enter into the spirit of it all and have all 20 aircraft ready as we needed them. The coordination would be incredible, and the chief weapons instructor, also my flight commander, bet me that it couldn't be done. That afternoon saw the squadron at its very best, and more than that, we could all see what each other was doing. In Germany, hardened shelter operations meant that you could only watch your own aircraft. The armament chief wore himself out coming backwards and forwards to make sure that his programme fitted ours. The weapons instructors worked flat out with a line of waiting room chairs for pilots waiting to have their films reviewed. My ops clerk thoughtfully provided magazines for them. And I felt like the sorcerer's apprentice longing for Merlin to come in and restore order.

It worked though and by five o'clock we had 20 successful gunnery sorties under the belt, and a good feeling to start the weekend. That was when some of us ended up in Newquay wondering what to do next. There was just the single night spot called 'Talk of the Town' featuring the well-named 'Last Chance Dance Band', but the following week who was appearing but Joe Brown and the Bruvvers? They were big in the 1970s. (Joe's farewell tour was in 2021). Joe didn't disappoint. He's a lovely person and a multi-talented musician, and he didn't know what to do in Newquay either. I discovered that after the show when I found myself sitting at a table next to him. Would he like to come up to St Mawgan and visit the squadron? Could he bring the Bruvvers? Would he bring the three-girl song and dance group called Valentine? It was all agreed and the next day I'd forgotten about it.

In the middle of the afternoon, probably a Friday, there was a call from the Guardroom. "Mr Brown and his band, says he's visiting 19 Squadron." We explained to the boss what a good idea this was and a great visit was had by all. Joe invited us to the Talk of the Town that evening and had two stage-side tables reserved. He and the girls performed as if the rest of the room didn't exist. It was the highlight of the

The singer and musician Joe Brown and his band during their visit to RAF St Mawgan posing with members of 19 Squadron. Joe is in the Phantom's front cockpit, while the author stands at centre on the ground, wearing sunglasses.

deployment. It is hard to remember anything else that happened. We finished the gunnery. Everyone qualified and we had made a number of friends at RAF St Mawgan, leading up to our departure party. Everyone on arrival was offered a 'Blue Dolphin' – the squadron's cocktail. In fact, this was its introduction. It tasted wonderful, and in this atmosphere one of the WRAF air traffic controllers presented us with a large blue and white chequered dolphin, mentioned previously. Now, the squadron crest was a Chinese killer dolphin chosen when the world was new, to reflect the Sopwith Dolphin flown by 19 Squadron. Hers, though, was Flipper, but no matter. It was the thought that counted, and the obvious hard work during her free time.

At some point the decision was made that the dolphin would have to fly back to Germany, next decision supersonic, and another decision in a diamond nine formation. They asked me, as the aerodynamicist, what happened to a shock wave in formation, did everyone hide behind the leader or what? I thought about our supersonic intercept work and said I didn't think it mattered, so the decision was made to do it anyway. The next morning, of course, was the Cornish monsoon, so the formation briefed for a stream take-off where each aircraft would only move once the runway water had subsided. One aircraft was unserviceable and I seem to remember that the interval between aircraft was over a minute. Certainly, when I was finally airborne, Radar said that our leader was coasting out over the east coast. We finally made it into a fairly rough diamond before we got into Dutch airspace.

"Gate, Gate, Go." This was the leader calling for afterburner, everyone's lit up, and we pushed the formation up to around Mach 1.2. "Parks, look, a supersonic Diamond Nine," this to my dear friend and navigator Tony Parker, sadly no longer with us. I got a loud snore over the intercom and I could then see him in the mirrors, fast asleep in the rear cockpit. To the day he passed, he never believed that the supersonic diamond nine had happened, and that we had christened the dolphin, Dolly for short.

A POLICE DOG'S DINNER

Well, it was a dark and stormy night on Battle Flight, with Christmas approaching fast. This was 19F Squadron at RAF Wildenrath at the end of 1978. Battle Flight, as we know, involved two fully armed F-4s on 24-hour five-minute readiness. So around ten o'clock at night, the ground crew were muttering that it was my turn to make the tea, possibly correct, so while I shook out the dregs onto the grass, there, outside our shelter, stood a drenched young corporal (acting unpaid) with a very sorry-looking large German Shepherd. I called him over and asked him to bring his handler along for a mug of tea.

So, as they shivered and started to thaw out, the ground crew scooped up all the dinner leftovers of curry and rice that filled the washing-up bowl. The animal wolfed it all down, and started to chase the bowl around the room to get the last drop. Then with a great sigh he then collapsed in front of the telly, paws in the air and started to snore. He was massive. We measured him from nose tip to tail end at well over 2 m. In the end, of course, his handler took his leave with a "Come on Satan" (or some such), "back to work". The dog went out muttering and we went back to Dutch telly.

About half an hour later, we heard a blood curdling: "HALT OR I RELEASE MY DOG." This was the first police challenge, the second being "HALT OR I FIRE". He never got that far. I looked out of the door expecting that we were under some form of attack, and there was the corporal (acting unpaid), straining towards the bushes with his mutt grinning up at him, wagging his tail and wondering if there was any more curry. Well, out of the foliage came a very wet and highly camouflaged police warrant officer who started a one-sided stream of abuse at the lad. I called him over, took the blame for ordering the youngster in for a tea, asked politely if he was able to spell my name and if he would be so good as to request access to a secure site next time he came. He turned out to be warrant officer dogs from the headquarters at RAF Rheindahlen, checking on the police dog patrols, and probably never had a sense of humour in his life. That was not the end of it though.

The next morning, I had 24 hours off, and at about 10.00 hours on the way home, I called in at the Guardroom to see the RAF Provost officer. We actually had two, but the senior copper was OK. "You're too late, he was here first thing. He charged the policeman and the dog, so I had to convene an orderly room [like a magistrate's court]." "How do you mean?" I asked quite innocently. "Well, you can imagine that your name featured quite a bit in the evidence. For looking after our lad, you have now achieved hero status amongst my RAF policemen, but I had to give him three days confined to barracks." That was the absolute minimum punishment possible. "Please don't do it again."[8]

"There's more, I'm afraid," he went on. "He charged the dog as well." "You're joking, what did you give him?" "Two weeks' bread and water to make him fierce again." "Oh dear, I am sorry about that." "There's worse," said the Provo. "He's reduced to the ranks. He was a fine Sergeant Airdog, and I had to take away his tapes." He'd loved his curry though. The dog must have passed on now, but I still feel really bad about the lad.

IN THE LEVANT

At last, we were tasked with an armament practice camp at RAF Akrotiri on the south coast of Cyprus, for a month's air-to-air gunnery. Like the APCs at RAF St Mawgan, the format would be similar, with three Canberras to tow the target flags and four firing slots a day under the Mount Olympus fighter control. We used the Gatling SUU-23A 20-mm cannon as our weapon of choice which was slowed down from 6,000 to 4,000 rounds per minute. A short burst that was still a lot of bullets. Each aircraft carried solid rounds, dipped in different colours of powder paint, so that hits could be counted against a keenly contested ladder and a NATO qualifying score.

The minimum angle off was 15 degrees, deemed to keep the Canberra safe, but the Canberra crews still managed to entertain with stories of how close the bullets had passed. Every film was meticulously viewed by the squadron weapons instructors,

8 Three days of restrictions was the minimum punishment possible, but essential to avoid the possibility of double jeopardy later on.

actually looking for improvement as well as fouls. A moustache-growing competition was usually run in parallel with the gunnery, where mine was magnificent, and lasted about ten minutes after I got home.

The main differences from St Mawgan were that the base opened from 07.00 to 14.00, and you could go for a swim afterwards without fear of exposure from the cold. Uniform, if not flying suit, was khaki shirt and shorts. There was always plenty to do, taxis were cheap and dinner away from base was an exotic Greek or Turkish 'cuisine'. This was some years before the Russian infiltration and the rampant housing development on both sides of the island. Paphos was then at the end of a long potholed dirt road, and consisted of a restaurant, a 'Cypriot Delight' factory (Turkish Delight of course), two pelicans and Pontius Pilate's villa from when he was governor. Wine was primitive and plentiful, but fine if it didn't burn the plastic tablecloth.

The squadron deployment in June 1979 went well, with a very early morning start to make the 14.00 closure. Routing was two hours to Brindisi, an Italian joint user airfield near the heel of Italy, with our new friends from Grazzanise to help

Armament practice camp line-up at RAF Akrotiri.

No. 19 Squadron at RAF Akrotiri for armament practice camp.

see us through. A ground crew party had deployed the previous day to service the Phantoms as we transited in four aircraft waves. This was a Wednesday, and after the ground crew had removed the Phantom's external fuel tanks, gunnery started the next day. "Al, you're running the desk." "Oh no. I've done this for the last two years. It's someone else's turn. I'm taking some leave." It was then Dave Pyper's turn to refuse the honour, and we determined to make ourselves scarce with a trip to the Holy Land. The squadron engineering officer, John Gilbert, decided that it would do his new junior a power of good to be left in charge under the stern eye of the engineering warrant officer and the mercy of the armourers. New boss, Wing Commander Tim Gauvain, capitulated.

And that's what we did, with a Cyprus Airways BAC-111 flight from Larnaca to Tel Aviv and a limo into Jerusalem. At some point it was decided that Dave would act as treasurer and that he would ask us for money as he needed it. John would act as tour manager and make sure that we visited everywhere we'd ever heard of. My job would be entertainments officer, to decide where we took meals and what we did in the evenings. The only rule was no argument, and it worked perfectly. We still haven't argued about it to this day.

We spent a morning in the souk in Jerusalem, where I bought a sheepskin coat for my small son. The transaction took two hours, sitting cross legged on the concrete floor, starting with the currency we would bargain in. I figured (wrongly) that the stall holder would be less confident in Deutschmarks. We then eventually agreed on a price, after numerous cups of mint tea, which a tour guide later told us would have been what a downtown store might have charged. Even the Eurocheque was presented the next day. John did us proud. We took a tour to Galilee via Jericho. We walked round all the holy places in Jerusalem, and we marvelled at the Wailing Wall and the Tomb of Abraham, where the world's religions merge. We went to Bethlehem under armed guard.

We travelled out to the Dead Sea for a float on the surface, covered with black chemical mud, and felt almost too floppy to take the cable car up to the ancient Masada fortress, where the Zealots held out against a Roman army for three years. Our guide quietly read out the words of their leader choosing death before slavery before initiating their mass suicide. It was relayed to the Romans apparently by two women who had hidden in the cavernous water cisterns. The Romans called it a victory, so maybe their politicians were not too different to ours. So, exhausted from cultural overload and quite broke, the fun was not quite over. At Tel Aviv Airport we met the security manager who introduced his cohort of really lovely girls, all dressed in white cotton blouse and blue jeans, and all veterans from the Israeli army. Security included a body search in a discrete cubicle, where one was very much aware that she could kill you with her little finger. The security manager was waiting on the other side. "What did you think of our security?" "Awesome. Can we go round again please?" A firm "No you can't". It wasn't quite over, as Cypriot immigration was not prepared to put an entry stamp in our passports dated after the exit stamp. They realised that by arriving at Akrotiri we had beaten the system, and eventually they let us out through a back door, passports unstamped.

The air-to-air shooting went well, the social life went like a holiday, and John took back control of the engineers. The armourers were the stars as ever, and we celebrated with a squadron photograph and a diamond nine formation flypast. The base was totally unimpressed, and as we left for the long flight back to Germany, they prepared themselves for the next squadron arriving the following day!

A couple of months later, I received a posting to the Phantom 228 OCU at RAF Coningsby. Time was running out, when I was offered what we called a 'Southern Ranger', the opportunity to take a pair of fighters unsupported to RAF Akrotiri for the weekend. I guess this was a simulated re-enforcement capability, but it was fun anyway. Again, it was an early start, on this occasion because of peacetime manning Akrotiri closed at 14.00 local time, two hours ahead of Germany. We checked with Grazzanise and they would be unable to acquire sufficient fuel for the outbound leg but could take us on the return flight. We opted for a turn-round at Brindisi, a massive airfield where the Italians based a squadron of Fiat G.91s, but were happy to help with turn-rounds. All went well.

Now, in our baggage pods, as well as spare chutes and oils, we were also carrying some cases of Dolphin wine, actually a rather nice Moselle in litre bottles, with its label adapted to our squadron crest. Imagine our surprise when we were met by two pilots from the Decimo Gruppo, who had flown over in their F-104s to ensure our trouble-free passage. "We 'ave brought you da spider wine!" We had drunk gallons of the stuff at Grazzanise and when we discovered a spider drowned inside a bottle, we called it 'spider wine', or '*Vino Bianco di Ragno*'. Right there on the blistering tarmac we exchanged boxes of wine. We flew on. At Akrotiri, we were met by Sandy Davies, a highly charismatic flight commander on 23 Squadron with, "Hurry up, Friday Happy Hour's starting in a few minutes. What have you got to contribute?" We contributed the spider wine, and had a fairly indulgent weekend, in which I imagine windsurfers and mezes featured. We invested in a couple of demijohns of Commandaria (OK, Cypriot Communion wine) and I retrieved a pair of patent leather mess boots that I had ordered and forgotten about.

On the Monday there was a westerly jet stream howling down the Med, the Brits weren't speaking to the Greeks, and so Crete was a viable alternate airfield only in extreme emergencies. We crossed fingers and set off to Brindisi. However, there was still a small chance that if we had sufficient fuel at the Italian airspace boundary, we might just be able to continue to Grazzanise. I had briefed accordingly. And we had! How do you change your destination? Like this:

"Brindisi, on best available forecast we have filed for Lima India Bravo Bravo, but our preferred destination is Lima India Romeo Mike. Request new destination."

"RAFAIR, now let me get this straight. You no like to land Brindisi but like to land Grazzanise. You descend Level One Five Zero."

"Negative descend, we don't have the fuel and request remain level Three One Zero."

"RAFAIR, you like to land Grazzanise, you descend One Five Zero. You like to fly Three One Zero, you land Brindisi."

"Request very slow rate descent."

"Approved."

There were no alternate airfields across the whole of southern Italy, as we slid down to 15,000 feet watching the fuel vanish. Finally, Rome Control cleared us to Grazzanise. "You make the TACAN One descent." That would take us a further 100 miles with an enormous tear drop out to sea. I could see Naples Airport out to the left in 50 miles visibility, and Grazzanise straight ahead. "RAFAIR Speedbrakes and NATO Six GO", the common approach frequency. We got told to make the TACAN One as we hurtled earthwards. "RAFAIR NATO Two GO". That's common tower, and again the same instruction. By this time, we're at 1,000 feet with a few miles to run. "Request pitch direction." "OK right pitch."

When we walked in, they'd gone to lunch some time ago, not believing that we could have flown more than two and a half hours. The pilot left manning the desk asked: "What you do? Napoli very angry." I told the story. He then explained that Naples 'owned' the airspace through which we'd descended and Rome had no communications with them. He flicked down one of the six comms switches he had to the outside world, and had a long, heated exchange with Naples ATC. He then turned to us with: "I explain to Napoli and say that you are nice people, and they say OK." We had lunch, exchanged our Commandaria for more spider wine, and flew home. I finally understood Joseph Heller's *Catch-22* where Milo Minderbinder got into Mediterranean trading.

I flew four more times with 19 Squadron, including a weapons cross-servicing flight to the Americans at Hahn. Then we packed up our beloved duty-free Peugeot 504, exchanged headlights with the incoming padre, and went on a short skiing holiday to Laax in Switzerland. This was vital in order to have owned the car for a year. HM Customs man at Dover was quite sharp. He found the box of cigars under the seat and tutted for a bit, then went through my diary a page at a time. 365 days out of Britain exactly since the car was bought, so he counted again to make sure. Welcome home.

CHAPTER SIX

BATTLE FLIGHT SCRAMBLE

"BATTLE FLIGHT SCRAMBLE" 2 AUGUST 1978

And we're off, running into our hardened shelter and our fully armed F-4. We're taxiing two minutes later, still winding up the second engine, with Stu Black, my back-seater, handling the radar and reading out pre-take-off vital actions. The local controller is passing the rest of the scramble order, essentially to head for the East German border at max speed and any height. Two minutes and 40 seconds was the fastest scramble ever recorded at RAF Wildenrath, part of RAF Germany in 1978.

A few minutes ago, we were sitting quite peacefully in the little bungalow next to the Phantom's hardened shelter. Stu was concentrating on one of his lovely aircraft watercolours and I'm now ashamed to admit I had my feet up, talking on the phone and smoking a NAAFI small cigar. Our three ground crew were in the next room playing cards. In the background the telebrief was making its eternal 'tic-toc' noises, which indicated that the line to ops and then sector was open. So, when a German voice suddenly called the scramble, we were gone. At the same time the RAF ops officer in the hardened ops bunker set off a siren, several sets of traffic lights and opened the shelter doors.

For the ground crew this is a well-oiled procedure, one of them starting the ground power generator, and the other two following us up the ladders to help us strap in, at the same time as I start the right engine. Generator online, helmet connected, seat pins stowed, INS running, ground crew pulling the chocks, and we're moving, at the same time starting the left engine. End of the runway now, scramble order acknowledged, cleared for take-off, checks complete, the afterburners lit and we're passing 100 knots. Then lift off, gear and flaps retracted and at around 300 knots we turn hard right for the border.

We check in with Clutch Radar and then we're crossing over Düsseldorf at 10,000 feet, still accelerating and passing Mach 1.2. Then it's over to 'Loneship', a German air force fighter control site on the NATO common fighter frequency. They tell us that our target is 50 miles ahead, slow speed and low level, a suspected helicopter. We descend, still fast, all eight missiles armed and the Gatling ready. We make a decision to maintain medium speed in order to manoeuvre if needs be and accelerate to the Phantom's cornering speed of 420 knots.

At 2,000 feet above the Hartz Mountains, Stu has the target on radar. As we close, we can see that it is in fact a light aircraft heading south-east, in all probability taking a shortcut across the prohibited border, but we're not taking chances. There could still be an armed helicopter following behind, so we settle on 300 knots. About now we are passed to 'Backwash', the next fighter control site, and we report the target. I make the first pass on his left with a 200-knot overtake, identify the aircraft as a four-seat Cessna, then put on 90 degrees of left bank to show him the weapons. We can only imagine his reaction and have a chuckle as we make a hard 360-degree right turn for a second pass. This time I manage to get the first two letters of his registration, but Stu is quite unable to get a picture.

We make three more passes to get the full registration and for Stu to get his picture. We are passed on to Cedar Mine, in the American-controlled half of the

The light aircraft that caused the scramble alert.

NATO Central Region, and amazingly it is seamless. Then when Sector Control is satisfied that this really is just an idiot breaking the law, we get sent home. No urgency this time, and we make a sedate climb to altitude with normal air traffic procedures. Then Stu says, "Do you think I spilt the water on my painting?" I say, "Well let's just hope that it spilt over my cigar". After landing, we shut down in front of our hardened shelter and our ground crew push the aircraft back for a turn-round servicing. Half an hour later we're ready to go again as lunch arrives. We heard much later that the offending pilot was fined and his licence confiscated. By chance I also met the German air traffic control supervisor whose dry comment was, "A Battle Flight scramble is a national Mayday call. I made a big hole over Düsseldorf and you went through the middle. Don't worry about broken windows; the federal government probably sent a man round with a bag of gold to pay for them."

Air defence was unlike any other form of military flying, in that when the 'scramble' came, the crew never knew what they would face. Scrambles were constantly practised on exercises, but of course Battle Flight was real, with air and ground crews totally qualified, fit and trained. So, we trained minutely at every bit of the operational envelope, including intercepts at all heights and speeds, then in exercises where this was all put together, plus various deployments for weaponry and air combat training.

The normal air-defence week probably started on the Friday when the boss, the squadron commander, would have the full programme for the week ahead, the flight commanders would work out aircraft availability with the engineers and then the deputy flight commanders would translate this into a flying programme. This would take into account Battle Flight rostering, simulator training, medicals, annual leave and so on. Visitors were invariably a feature of Germany life and I well remember talking at length over a coffee to a fascinating man with an Astrakhan hat, who called me "Comrade" and turned out to be George Brown, Harold Wilson's right-hand man.

Practice intercepts were of course the bread and butter of the job. Much of this would be at low level, where peacetime restrictions gradually made training more difficult as the German public became more resistant to aircraft noise. Peacetime airspace restrictions meant that fighters could not use the preferred heights for fighter patrol, were limited on speed and banned from using afterburner below 3,000 feet. It was highly restrictive, unrepresentative of any wartime requirement and often frustrating. There were very strict rules on engaging with targets of opportunity, tactical aircraft of other air forces, though in fairness rules gradually relaxed and became more realistic.

All that said, tearing around Germany at 420 knots at 250 or 500 feet above the ground was massive fun, and we did it most days. Any such activity in the Netherlands was totally banned but we were rather more welcome over Belgium, where not a lot had changed since 1945. In fact, in the 1970s the requirement for mixed fighter force air defence gradually evolved with the RAF frequently operating with the Belgians or the Dutch, using the best of each other's capabilities. We were highly aware that while, at the time, our equipment was superior in quality to the opposition's, there was a vast disparity in numbers.

Air combat training was difficult in Germany with the embargo on supersonic flight and the need to carry significant recovery fuel. The answer was increasingly a few weeks at the air combat manoeuvring range at Decimomannu. Instrumented buoys, anchored out to sea, measured the exact parameters of all participating fighters, so that on a trigger pull, a simulated 'kill' could be awarded or denied. The combat sorties were quite intricate, evaluating set up tactics as well as all-out warfare with the other participating air forces, notably the American F-15s, with absolutely no speed or noise restrictions.

Too much fun? Maybe, but German night and all-weather flying brought back reality. Of course, we had to practise supersonic intercepts, often at night, and indeed supersonic flight was permitted above 36,000 feet. High-level intercepts were another type of problem, demanding very accurate handling and speed control. Night visual identifications were another real 'test of character' with visual identification of a lights-out target and night close formation (with lights out maybe the hardest flying I have ever attempted). And of course, the German winter itself made demands for extreme instrument flying accuracy.

We did get to know our NATO allies through weapons cross-servicing, where we might take a pair of F-4s to a German or American F-4 base, so that their armourers could practise loading their own weapons onto our aircraft. Incidentally, the US Navy's Sparrow loaded directly onto an RAF (navy derived) F-4. The USAF's Sidewinder needed special umbilical cords. We had annual squadron exchanges where half the squadron would deploy to another NATO base for a fortnight, getting to know the crews and flying with them. Taking four Phantoms over the bowl of Mount Etna was unforgettable. We would frequently meet other NATO crews at various fly-ins or fighter meets, gradually developing long-term understanding, friendship and trust. A NATO beer call was an 'at-home' when a wing offered open house to all comers. The Germans at Nörvenich even made the RAF and USAF visitors crawl in through a tunnel.

Everything came together on the occasional exercise, either national or on a grander scale, sometimes lasting a week. Often the targets never stopped, with every shot claimed carefully measured on film. Once a quarter the base put its own crews through the wringer, with particular emphasis on ground defence, even under gas or nuclear conditions. Annually RAF Germany held a large-scale exercise, and also annually each base received a tactical evaluation from a NATO team. The results were highly competitive.

So, there we were, on 2 August 1978, descending fast, back down through 10,000 feet, looking for our target. We had practised the scramble many times, as had our ground crew. We knew the air traffic procedures thoroughly, as well as the interface with fighter control. We had practised with the German fighter controllers many times. We knew the limitations of the AWG-12 radar intimately in picking out low-level contacts, and we had no illusions about intercepting a slow speed target. We knew the rules of engagement and we understood the likely usefulness of each weapon against something like a light aircraft (in fact we had selected the Gatling cannon as the weapon of choice). We understood the dynamics of manoeuvring around a slow speed target, and we trusted each other totally.

In the end, it was just another day in the life of an air-defence fighter crew doing their bit for the Cold War. We won though, didn't we?

CHAPTER SEVEN

NATO PARTNERS

THE GERMANS – FIGHTER CONTROL, SECTOR 2 UEDEM, 1976

As a part of the Bonn–Paris conventions of the 1950s, air defence of West Germany was created as four sectors. The British would run Sector 1 in Niedersachsen (Lower Saxony) and Sector 2 at Goch in Nord Rhein-Westphalen, near RAF Laarbruch. The Americans would run Sector 3 to the south, and the French Sector 4 over Bavaria (later merged with Sector 3). Each sector was responsible for NATO's command and control of radars, fighters and surface-to-air missiles (SAMs). In 1976, some of the systems were distinctly dated and the chances of friendly fire in wartime were increasing.

We were outnumbered about six to one by our Cold War opposition, so the argument was always quality against quantity. Every shot would have to count, but new weapons systems were on their way, starting with the RAF's contribution of a very small fighter wing equipped with Phantoms, having an ability to see targets at low level. General Sir John Hackett, one of the British NATO commanders, later described the situation brilliantly in his analyses *The Third World War* and its sequel *The Third World War: The Untold Story.* I had a briefing slide reminding us that 'Custer died in a target rich environment'.

Up in the bunker near Goch, at a site called Uedem, 'Sector 2' was behind a glass screen ready to control the air battle, which for them at the time meant the Belgian

F-104 fighter wing at Beauvechain and a reasonable number of SAMs. These were in practice the NIKE high-level SAM and the HAWK for medium- to low-levels, operated by the Germans, Dutch and Belgians. The HAWK was an American system, which they said meant, 'Homing All the Way Killer'. The Germans said it meant '*Heute Alle Wieder Kaput*', meaning 'Today everything is once again broken'.

In front of the glass were the German national fighter controllers in one of a dozen or so ground control intercept (GCI) sites, of which ours answered to 'Crabtree'. We had started working with them at medium and high levels, and we were getting curious about who they were, while they were increasingly excited about having their 'own' fighter wing to play with. It was clearly time for a visit. An RAF coach was organised and best uniforms were the order of the day. When we first arrived at Wildenrath, we really had no idea what to expect. We found out later that the national side of the glass rarely spoke to the NATO side because the Germans employed in NATO jobs were entitled to duty-free.

What we didn't expect was steam coming out of the coach ventilation grills, as it blew its cylinder head gasket miles from anywhere in the middle of the rather bleak Westphalian countryside. Nobody on the coach had a word of German but the driver had the Wildenrath phone number and with much sign language we persuaded a suspicious farmer's wife to let us use her phone. The driver at least had some idea where we were, but a replacement bus would take a couple of hours. That was how we arrived two hours late at the GCI site where our German hosts were starting to get ready to go home. We learned the hard way that you are *never* late for a German invitation; not a great start to our new relationship.

A Luftwaffe Oberstleutnant (lieutenant colonel) was in charge and was clearly very annoyed. We dismissed him as a wingless useful idiot, but in fairness he caught up an hour with a high speed conducted tour lasting around ten minutes. They had laid out a very generous spread for us when we arrived at their *Offizierheim* (officers' mess); it was all very tense though and conversation was stilted. It was made fairly clear that the visit was an international disaster. Those of us who had come from 29 Squadron, though, had the answer, and persuaded the German barman to concoct a 'chocolate spider'. The Germans were frankly amazed by the sight of a one-litre beer glass full of something that actually sizzled and tasted so nice. Some of those just leaving sensed a change in the air and came back in as the rules were explained; that this was a drink of pure friendship which you sipped and passed on. It may have been that they were in a second language but a number of them gulped down as much as possible before rushing outside. They were hooked.

The Oberstleutnant explained their operational final check was called 'Traffic Lights', where three 30-ml glasses of a light beer were lined up, one laced with cherry brandy, one with advocaat, and one with crème de menthe. They looked beautiful, had to be drunk very fast in that order, and tasted awful. Nobody was exempt. We responded with a round of *Ratzeputz*, a totally disgusting local schnapps made of ginger, which we told them was a brandy "down in one" and the evening gently deteriorated.

The Oberst (colonel) arrived having previously decided to boycott, and joined in enthusiastically, then the RAF bus arrived to take us home. The Oberst grandly dismissed the driver and announced that we would leave when he was ready. Mike Stephenson, a young navigator recently engaged, suddenly realised that he would miss his engagement party and was last seen running after the bus. He missed it of course and held the grudge for months afterwards. She forgave him. I found myself talking to a veteran pilot in the corner of the bar who had survived the war. The Oberstleutnant was furious. "We do not talk to him. He is from former times and we are obliged to have him as an officers' mess member." Lesson learned, but he was still cross about the *Ratzeputz*.

Late into the evening, a German coach arrived and we were poured into it, with promises of friendship for life. When we walked into the bar at Wildenrath an hour later, we clashed with a Harrier Wing Ladies Guest Night and were immediately banished. It transpired that our main offence was that everyone had a black knot where their RAF black ties should have been. The Germans had cut our ties off as a part of our operational check out.

We had them back to Wildenrath later with wives in attendance, but it wasn't the same. They were spot on time and had even been briefed on the rules for the chocolate spider.

NATO BEER CALL, 20 APRIL 1977

Maybe the less said about the Great NATO Beer Call the better. We'd newly arrived on the scene, so it was time to invite the neighbours for a housewarming party. The new station commander, John Mitchell, needed little persuasion. There was a great history of NATO beer calls, although not quite so many recently perhaps, but it seemed to be a good idea to invite all of the air-defence wings, the other RAF stations, and the fighter controllers to a hangar party where they would get to know us and have a great evening.

Invitations went out to all points of the compass, but we had little idea who might come, apart from various inbound aircraft movements. One such was even from the French. A hangar was requisitioned, normally used for storing vehicles, and the NAAFI manager was given carte blanche for food and drink supplies. We also bribed him with his own flying suit (the one with three weatherproof NAAFI trading stamps on each shoulder, since he was apparently a captain in the NAAFI Reserve. Who knew?) An enormous skip arrived plus two scrap Volkswagens and a number of pianos to put in it. Dress would be flying suits, and hard luck if you didn't own one.

On the appointed day, a large number of fighters arrived in the course of the afternoon, German, American, Canadian and various others. Then as evening approached the coaches started to arrive, mainly Dutch and Belgians, including large contingents from our friends at Leeuwarden and Beauvechain. Everyone spoke English and the party was off to a flying start. Battle Flight was scrambled at one point to make a fast and noisy low flypast before departing on a border patrol.

Nobody had noticed the large contingent of German fighter controllers standing rigidly in their best uniforms, looking a little self-conscious. We discovered afterwards that they had never previously been invited to anything, and their general had ordered representatives from all the fighter control sites to attend. This was too much for the Dutch, who grabbed a fire extinguisher and went straight down their line. One German stood his ground muttering: "If I had known what this would be like, I would have worn my father's SS uniform and brought my Dobermann dog." He exchanged his soggy uniform for a flying suit.

The Dutch had to be restrained from playing skittles with their beer mugs on the grounds that they would have nothing to drink from, and some Germans had to be coaxed down from the ceiling crane where they were busy removing all the national flags. Flying suits were exchanged, the pianos were set on fire and then the two Volkswagens. A blazing Volks was pushed into the giant skip, the sides went white hot, and the hangar door buckled. A French pilot was using pure bladder pressure to attempt to drill a hole in the side of the blazing skip. That was it really. The beer was turned off, the lights extinguished and almost everyone went to bed, that is apart from the navigator who found himself the other side of the Dutch border wearing an orange German flying suit, with no idea how he got there.

The next day was a clear up day and the visiting aircraft departed in the afternoon. The skip was a mess and the hangar door never closed properly again. The rubbish contractor accepted a five per cent monthly payment for the skip added to the rubbish bill over the rest of the station commander's tour, but, horror, the NATO national flags were missing. These had been borrowed from the NATO land headquarters at Sittard, so a signal was sent to all asking for them back. A German Phantom landed the next day and taxied past the air traffic control tower. Then the back canopy opened and the back-seater stood up and threw a bundle of flags out of the aircraft. Well, we had certainly arrived. Everyone knew who we were by now, so I guess it was a great success.

I saw John Mitchell again in 2009, now an air commodore. My dear friend Hylton Price had been killed in the tragic mid-air collision between two RAF Grob 115 Tutors. Rob van de Pol and his wife came over from the Netherlands and Wendy and I flew down to St Athan in our Europa. Hylton had been to stay with Rob in Dutch Friesland and Rob had been at Hylton's wedding. We had been good friends. John Mitchell paled when he saw Rob at the wake as the beer call flashed before his eyes. There were the makings of another great party were it not such a desperately sad occasion.

THE DUTCH – SQUADRON EXCHANGE WITH 322 SQUADRON RNLAF, F-104S, AGAIN

It had to be the spring, maybe the summer, of 1978. We had been drawn to exchange with, would you believe, our opposite numbers on 322 Squadron, Royal Netherlands Air Force, our friends from the 29 Squadron exchange from RAF Coningsby. This time I was to be on the home team, but we had their phone numbers. We had quietly sorted out who would exchange at Leeuwarden and who would be at Wildenrath. So, it wasn't really a surprise when a number of familiar faces arrived at Wildenrath with four F-104Gs and ground crew. Flying and alcohol were clearly on the agenda (consecutively), and actually we were good about not mixing them. I have a note that I had taken the squadron engineering officer to Leeuwarden in September 1978, so maybe that had been a part of the preparation. In passing, the cross-servicing flight at Leeuwarden was like a miniature Science Museum. They had apparently 'borrowed' every special tool for every NATO type since the re-establishment of the Royal Netherlands Air Force.

It was good to see the familiar faces, including my dear friend Rob van de Pol. Caes van Waart was there, whom I've seen many times since, and Dick Berlijn who became the chief of the Dutch air staff. I don't remember flying with them, but we must have done. The big event planned was a weekend in Brussels, via some beers with 349 Squadron, Belgian air force, at Beauvechain near Louvain. Many of the Belgian pilots had trained with the Dutch. Two of the Belgians then came with us into Brussels, where we stayed in the Belgian officers' club. We then spent the Saturday firmly based in *Le Chaloupe d'Or*, or Golden Hind, a brasserie located with a view of the Grande Place, and former headquarters of the Tailors' Guild, making excursions into the city throughout the day.

It all ended in a glorious dinner in one of the many restaurants with a family from Luxembourg who thought they might like to join in. In fact, we decided to kid the new boss who didn't quite trust us to take care of things. He clearly mistrusted me to run the event since the flight commander had diverted that afternoon. The landlord agreed to a 'spoof' bill for thousands of Belgian francs. Halfway through the evening he announced that we'd spent that, so what would we like to do now? We put a zero on the end and carried on. Then there was the somewhat quieter bus trip back to Wildenrath (I do remember everyone getting out of the bus to relieve themselves on the roadside, when the driver then moved the bus forwards).

The weekend wrapped up with a heroes' return to 19 Squadron and a grand family lunch. It had been a great success. We presented the bill to the new boss with a vague explanation that it hadn't been paid, but the embassy was involved, as well as the Dutch military attaché. It was explained over the next hour that it included the cost of the grand piano, pushed out of the window. Even so …but it fell on the landlord's car. New boss saw his career coming to a sharp ending until the missing South African flight commander, Graeme Smith, whom I admired, heard the Dutch discussing it. Of course, he understood Afrikaans, and the game was over.

The following day, Monday, I was on Battle Flight. The Dutch had three F-104s flying. The first we knew about an accident was a call from ATC that the runway was blocked. We had then to think seriously about a scramble, if necessary, from Wildenrath's parallel southern taxiway. It just needed forethought. Then we heard that two F-104s had collided on the runway. Then we discovered that Hennie Alberson, Dutch pilot and veteran of the Brussels trip, was dead.

Hennie had told us that he was getting a divorce from his lovely wife, who some of us had met. He would finalise this the following week. Maybe his mind wasn't on the landing. On the F-104 control column there was a multi-function button that could make a radio transmission in the air or work the nose wheel steering on the ground. For some reason Hennie was landing third in a stream, and was too close to the aircraft in front. The accident board picked out the 'clicks' in attempted radio transmissions so maybe the switch failed to change function. We never found out. Hennie collided with the aircraft in front. (Normally we landed on one side of the runway and then moved over to leave a side clear.) The tailplane of the second aircraft had gone through Hennie's cockpit and into Hennie. Our friend was beyond recovery. The remaining two aircraft and the rest of the Dutch left before the end of the week. It was all desperately sad.

We went to Hennie's funeral. Our station commander arranged a Pembroke from 60 Squadron to take maybe eight of us to Leeuwarden, himself, myself, and others who felt close to Hennie and to the Dutch. The fighter gods arranged appalling weather over Friesland and we duly lined the route into the church in rain-soaked best blue uniform, RAF totally merged with the RNLAF. The four-aircraft 'missing man' formation was cancelled even after the aircraft had taxied, and as Hennie's coffin was carried towards the church a single F-104 appeared in the clouds and rain, then vanished upwards in full afterburner. It wrung emotion from even the most hard-bitten fighter pilot, and was the right way to say goodbye. Fighter flying is relentless and unforgiving.

There was a fairly intensive wake. Everyone was happy that because Hennie's divorce was not finalised, his widow would receive a full pension; a small compensation really, but it mattered. We then slept all the way back to Wildenrath. We'd seen Hennie off in grand style and that was what counted.

THE GERMANS – ASKING FOR HELP AFTER A BIRD STRIKE

It's July 1978, and a lovely clear day over the North German Plain for once. Noddy and I were down at 500 feet above the flat bit of Germany, where they say you can see on Saturday who's coming to lunch on Sunday. We're steady at 420 knots with our trusty wingman, actually a part-time staff officer, out at a mile on the right. We're coming up to the Dummer See, a large lake north of Osnabrück in Lower Saxony. We're happy, and we're off to make war on a pack of RAF Jaguars a bit further north still, and of course we're training for the real thing. Aren't we?

Then suddenly we're surrounded by hundreds of large angry seagulls, a long way from the sea but making a living in the marsh land south of the Dummer See. I've never been under fire (except by British Army tanks), but this was close. We heard multiple loud bangs all over the aircraft, and then we were through. Check the engine instruments, check the hydraulic gauges, feel the controls, and ease up away from the ground. We never forget that the ground has a probability of kill of 1.0. I call my No.

2 over and tell him what's happened. He can't stop giggling. "I can see right through your aircraft." "What do you mean?" I radio back in reply. "Like daylight, tee hee," he says. It's time to make a plan.

We're up at 2,000 feet now, doing around 250 knots with No. 2 in a loose formation. If we bail out, he wants the picture. Hopsten is a German air force Phantom base about 20 miles to the west with a good long runway and arrestor wires. We switch to Hopsten's radar director frequency. Now Brits are cool, and we don't make panicky radio calls.

"Hopsten", I radio, "this is Mike Lima Five Four, I have a small problem."

"Go ahead Mike Lima."

"We've had a multiple bird strike and considerable damage. We request a 15-mile straight-in approach and a priority landing."

Why 15 miles? Well, you never know what's going to happen, an engine might fail, the hydraulic oil might leak out, and full control might not be available.

"Mike Lima, maintain 2,000 feet, steer 270, you're No. 3 in the pattern."

"You don't understand. We have a damaged aircraft and need some priority."

"Negative Mike Lima, you do not understand. You are No. 3 in the bird strike pattern."

Who says Germans don't have a sense of humour?

We found out after landing that No. 1 was a Danish J35 Draken, and No. 2 was one of Hopsten's own F-4F Phantoms. Probably the gulls had been initially disturbed by someone flying fast and low, for which the German air force RF-4E Phantoms from Leck in Schleswig Holstein were the usual suspects. The aircraft was a total mess, but this was before the days of camera phones so we never got a picture.

The German cross-servicing flight were their usual gruff welcoming selves, and we overdosed on coffee while Wildenrath diverted a 60 Squadron Pembroke in to Hopsten to collect us. Just the pilot and navigator were on board, and the nav gladly vacated the front seat to let me fly the Pembroke, with its two Alvis Leonides 127 nine-cylinder air-cooled radial engines, back to base under their pilot's watchful guidance. He happened to be their squadron QFI. The day ended with half an hour's circuits at Wildenrath until the fuel was all gone. An interesting day, with an unexpected bit of flying a new type. There was nothing special about the Pembroke except that I found it quite hard work.

The end of the tale? Not quite. The squadron had sent a repair team to Hopsten, who were quite happy to go. It was an adventure, a bit of a holiday with possibly extra allowances thrown in, led by the squadron warrant officer. A week later the aircraft was ready for collection, so guess who got the job? This time the army's 12 Flight obliged and we were flown up to Hopsten in one of their Gazelle AH-1 helicopters.

The Phantom was still a mess. The warrant officer had decided that this was a classic case for a battle damage repair. There were rivets sticking out of all the panels which had been roughly replaced, and two of the lads physically lifted the Perspex canopy and held it open while we got in. Of course, the Germans had air charging for canopy actuators, but being Brits, we had a non-standard 'standard NATO' fitting, and we ended up using aircraft power to charge it, five minutes on and five off in case it burnt out. The battery was flat, but amazingly a German power unit could be used to support electrics and start the aircraft.

The landing gear hydraulics were broken and we had no pressurisation, so we flew all the way back to Wildenrath at 250 knots with the gear down at 10,000 feet. For some reason the Welsh warrant officer thought it was all very funny. We had never detected any humour previously, so he'd clearly been learning from the Germans.

THE BELGIANS – FIRST BELGIAN F-16

I should caution the reader that nowhere in my pilot logbook is there a record of the intercept to which I shall now publicly confess. You may, however, become an accessory to the fact, and have problems with your EU visa.

It started with a routine pairs take-off from RAF Wildenrath's westerly runway, and the mission was a pretty straightforward session of practice intercepts with the Belgian fighter control at Glons, call sign 'Efflux'. However, between us and the training airspace over the Ardennes Forest there was a civilian airway. The easiest way to cross it was to make an afterburner climb in formation to 25,000 feet and cross over it, switching radio channel direct to Efflux. This was a demanding manoeuvre, particularly in cloud. However, one of my wingman's afterburners failed to light on take-off, and he decided to reject his take-off. (He was technically right of course.)

So, there we were at 25,000 ft checking in with a Belgian fighter controller.

"Efflux, this is Mike Lima Five Four, single aircraft."

"Mike Lima good morning, this is Efflux. Your No. 2 will not be joining us today, so we play 'Free Fighter'."

"No problem."

"We are on patrol."

Nothing has changed in the Belgian air force since the 1950s, and much of its fighter world is unchanged since D-Day. They were proud to be 'like the RAF was in 1945'. We loved them for it. We were paired operationally with the F-104 wing at Beauvechain, and 19 Squadron in particular with their 349 Squadron. They were great fun and good friends.

"Riser, Riser (straight from the 1950s code book). We have a bogie due north at 60 miles, Angels 20. Steer three five zero. Descend Angels one eight zero. Identify."

He means descend to 18,000 feet, make an intercept with a stern conversion and identify the target. My nav very quickly calculates the target heading and speed, and sets us up on a parallel reciprocal.

"Mike Lima Judy." Judy means that he now has control of the intercept. My job now is to fly quite accurately at a suitable speed, and before long I can see an aircraft where my nav is indicating. "Switches Safe." This is our bread and butter. We take it seriously and go through the drills for real.

"Starboard." That's my nav telling me to start a 45-degree turn to the right. "Roll out One Five Zero. Target is on the nose slightly high." Well, I can recognise an F-111E Raven silhouette now. He seems to be in the descent and he's pointing at the main American air base at Ramstein. No surprises there then. He's probably flown from one of the two F-111 bases in the UK, but home base would be Mountain Home, Idaho. Interesting. I close on him now at a modest overtake as we don't want to put him off. And then we're alongside.

"Target is friendly, F-111" and I read out his airframe number, waving at the pilot. He's been good enough to include 'Embellish' on his flight plan, meaning that he's prepared to act as an intercept target. He doesn't wave back.

"We are on patrol." Us. The team again. And we go round and round for what seems like a long time. Our radar is blank.

"We have the first Belgian F-16 on its delivery flight from the factory. Would you like to intercept?" Well, what would you have said? I said, "Roger".

"Ok, he's at low level over the Ardennes. I'll bring you in above him at 15,000 feet, then you take the Tally Ho!" This is a classic Belgian F-104 attack, where to make up for lack of turning ability, the fighter drops very steeply into the target's stern, giving him no time to manoeuvre. The Beauvechain pilots were pretty crazy and they made it work. And that's what we did. We could see the F-16A over the forest, nearly three miles below, and then we spotted the two F-104s a little way behind him in escort.

"Tally Ho!" It's like Judy for a visual engagement, as I roll upside down and pull the Phantom steeply down. We judge the F-16's speed to be around 420 knots, as we slide in behind him. The gun camera is on and I start filming this brand-new masterpiece. I see the two F-104s react in my mirrors but it is too late.

"Fox 3 F-16" I transmit, and at that moment a runway flashes underneath at right angles. Looking at the map, I suspect that it was probably Liège or possibly Sint-Truiden.

That evening, I get a telephone call at home from Hans Beyaert, a Belgian F-104 pilot and good friend from the Taceval team. They'd found out that I was the pilot. "Did you know that you flew over the saluting base where King Phillipe was taking the salute with the politicians and the generals?" "Ha ha." "It looked fantastic on the six o'clock news, and the reporter said that the British Royal Air Force had been kind enough to provide an escort." "How much trouble am I in?" "You're not. The air force have decided that you were doing your job exactly as we'd have expected of you. The Belgian fighter controller though is a traitor."

Well, nothing did happen, but we kept quiet about it. We didn't know the Belgian punishment for treason or if there was a statute of limitations. I never recorded the intercept in my logbook and to this day have no idea who the nav was. I did meet the controller though a few weeks later. He said that the air force were pretty cross with him, but he was retiring in three weeks and his pension was secure. "Did we have some fun though?" he asked. You bet we did.

THE ALLIES – BERLIN CORRIDOR REINFORCEMENT

At the end of the Second World War, Germany was divided into four administrations, British, American, French and Russian. Berlin sat in the Russian part, but was joined to the West by good road, rail and air links. Then in 1948 the Russians closed off the road and rail links, and would have sealed Berlin from the air. Berlin started to starve and the West quickly enabled re-enforcement by air. This culminated in an aircraft every 30 seconds in any weather, going in from the south or north and exiting west whether their load was delivered or not. Additionally, the RAF Sunderland flying boats were delivering salt onto Berlin's great Havelsee lake, near Gatow. Then in 1949 the Russians capitulated and ground contact was opened again. The Berlin Airlift is commemorated by the Berlin *Luftbrücke*, the start of the bridge outside Frankfurt Airport, and the finish just outside Tempelhof. It's poignant.

In case they should ever start again, a reinforcement exercise took place annually, running north to south along the Inner German Border in full view of the East German radars. Normally participants from the RAF, USAF and FAF congregated at RAF Gütersloh but this time they came to Wildenrath, a C-130 each from the RAF and USAF, a Transall from the French with USAF F-4Es from Hahn and Mirage IIIs from Colmar in Alsace. No. 19 Squadron made up the home team.

This amazing and irregular formation of the three transports and a gaggle of fighters flew daily and two varied fighters flew as enemy air, generally getting some shots away, on film of course. I flew one with a French pilot and we decided to use exact Soviet MiG-21 intercept tactics. We asked fighter control to bring us in on the beam, separated by 90 degrees or so, and supersonic. It was a disaster from our point of view and we were 'shot down' on each attack. The reinforcement package was learning.

The highlight of the exercise was the Sunday cricket match, where the British transport crews looked after the American and French fighter crews and we looked after their transporters. The rules were effectively tip and run, there was no restriction on alcohol (including the umpires); the teams were vast, so everyone had a go. We would have won if we could have persuaded our Americans not to drop the bat before they ran. In the evening the French were immaculately attired in best uniform and demonstrated opening champagne bottles with a fire axe then filled up glasses from foaming jagged bottles. The women were fascinated and most of them had to be dragged home.

For once the entente really worked.

THE ITALIANS – DECIMO GRUPPO, GRAZZANISE, MAY 1979

Our Italian squadron exchange in May 1979 turned out to be rather special, certainly a surprise. The Italians did not have a great reputation as social animals, and we knew nothing about their air force, except that they all wore expensive sunglasses. We had heard tales about non-stop shopping expeditions, and expected the worst. However, the Decimo Gruppo at Grazzanise just north of Naples was air defence like us, and flew the F-104G Starfighter. The climate was warm and sunny, the wine plentiful and, overall, it all sounded fine, apart from the shopping.

Stu Black and I taxied and got airborne before dawn, streaming as No. 2 in the four-ship. The logistics were complex, and we had to be away in time for our ground crew to pack and prepare for the Italians. The Italians would fly their ground crew to Wildenrath in a Douglas DC-7, which would then bring our team to Italy. They would arrive late, so we were fully prepared to do the after-flight servicing on the Phantoms. The ground crew were sceptical. Routing was over eastern France, since Austria didn't allow NATO overflights, so we were flying with three external fuel tanks, anticipating a flight of around two hours. One of my wing tanks refused to feed, and we started to think about possibly having to divert; no problem as there

In transit past Capri.

were plenty of airfields. However, as we turned south into Italy, the eastern rising sun probably melted ice around the fuel valve, fuel flowed and all was well. This had to be a good start to our ten days in Italy.

Grazzanise turned out to be a bare strip of concrete, with hangar and air traffic control, but not much more. We shut down in front of their squadron building, to be met by two of their pilots (big sunglasses), holding a tray of enormous goblets of red wine. We knew this one. "Welcome to Italy, may we offer you some local wine?" "Of course," went the reply. "We'll join you." "Wonderful, did you like that? Have another." "Thank you. We'll join you." Well, we had diverted from the script here, so we stood eye to eye until the tray was empty. The last two crews had given up waiting. It was a silly game of one-upmanship, but national pride was at stake. It turned out afterwards that the Italian shoppers had all gone to Wildenrath, and those remaining couldn't wait for the fun to start.

After a massive outdoor lunch in the sunshine, a snooze seemed to be in order; so much for the after-flight servicing. The evening ended in the officers' club bar with a tour of the many amarettos, and walking off arm in arm to indicate that honours were even and everyone was happy.

An Italian F-104 at Grazzanise.

The flying was a little different from our usual, starting the first few days with two-v-two low-level intercepts over the Tyrrhenian Sea around Ponza, which soon paled. After that we flew four-ships first into the Dolomites, then south down the Apennines, round Sicily and Mount Etna and back to the Bay of Naples. I was leading one of the flights approaching Sorrento, and had just called the formation to relax and move out, when a bright red Italian Macchi MB-326 went straight through the middle of the four. I met the pilot that evening, when the incident was quietly suppressed, but they did give me a trip in the Maachi. They kept the Maachi MB-326 on their station flight for pilots on ground tours to maintain basic currency. It certainly had a better performance than the Jet Provost Mk 5, but it was heavier on the controls. It responded well to aerobatics but it was clear that my Italian pilot was very wary of the vertical and possible spinning.

Our hosts had organised afternoon trips to Naples, Pompeii and Vesuvius, Caserta and the Isle of Capri, usually with a grand al fresco lunch. The pizza coined Decimo Gruppo times 19 Squadron was a disappointment though, as it turned out to be a 1-metre pizza and a 90-cm pizza instead of one large 190-cm pizza. The Tuesday also included a magnificent dinner in Naples. Our hosts were anxious to know if we had liked it all. “Yes, but where were the women?” “Oh no, we forgotta da wimmin.” The next evening was another dinner, this time with a wife, cousin, aunt or sister placed alternately with an Italian pilot in range to translate. It was a brilliant night. “You liked the dinner?" "Yes, but there was no dancing." "Oh no, we forgotta da dancing. You need a licence." So the next event was a dinner in the officers' club with a full female turnout, and a great time was had by all. Later that summer when I took Wendy and James back to Grazzanise, one of the Italian wives (husband had been in Wildenrath) told her, "I have been married 25 years, and this was the first time I ever went out without my husband." "So?" "I have just wasted 25 years."

After ten days everyone was ready for a rest. Our hosts organised a buffalo mozzarella cheese run to the local buffalo farm so that we were ready to start engines as soon as the cheese car appeared and the cheese was loaded into a baggage pod. In those days fresh buffalo mozzarella outside Naples was a rarity; indeed, the night train to Turin had refrigerated trucks so that the car workers' wives could buy it fresh in the morning. Our equivalent was an afterburner climb to above the freezing level. We continued this long afterwards when we would send a new pilot to Grazzanise for 'essential airways training', when he would get a good lunch, and come back with the fresh mozzarella.

That wasn't even the end of it. Our new friends had already recommended a safe sandy beach and a nice hotel to stay in, not far from Grosseto, maybe 250 km further north, suitable for a three-year-old to enjoy the seaside. I drove there in the summer with Wendy and James and it was all as they had said. After a week, we decided to visit

An Italian air force F-104 taking off from Grazzanise.

Rome before turning for home, and there on the Rome turn-off from the autostrada was a sign proclaiming Naples 120 km. Irresistible. Our Italian friends installed us in the officers' club, and came in every night for dinner. They then booked us into the Rome officers' club and arranged for us to use the MoD car park opposite, where the car would have an armed guard.

NOTE

Despite being the Decimo Gruppo (meaning a group of established individual traditional flights), they were also the 9° Stormo (literally a flock). Their antecedents had been closely involved with Ferrari, hence the Ferrari horse in their badge. That had led to their speciality of a nine-aircraft 'X' formation. There were a number of pictures on the walls of the X formation flying over the president and other dignitaries. They told us how it was done.

First of all, you need a 60-nautical mile approach in clear weather, where the nine aircraft are in a loose gaggle. The aircraft at the centre is the leader and he calls in the first two 'horns' of the X. When they are steady, he calls in the further pair, and then talks to them constantly. The trailing pairs are left to establish accurate symmetry with the usual step-down. The formation only had to be rock steady for a minute or so, and in the best traditions the formation runs the parade. Easy.

So, when they tried the St Andrew's Cross with only five Phantoms at Leuchars, they knew none of this. The leader was on one of the 'horns', and two aircraft collided. One crew ejected into the North Sea, and the other landed back in an aircraft that was subsequently a write-off. I asked the leader later, when he was cooling his heels in Germany, whether they knew the Italians' secret. "Listen," he said, "It was all right until we tried the barrel roll."

CHAPTER EIGHT

UK AIR DEFENCE

NO. 228 OCU AKA 64 (R) SQUADRON – IN THE BACK SEAT

No. 228 OCU was established in 1947 at RAF Leeming in Yorkshire, to train fighter and light-bomber crews on the Mosquito, Meteor and then the Javelin FAW.5, when it specialised in all-weather and night-fighter training until it disbanded in 1961. As we know, it was reformed at RAF Leuchars from 1965 to 1966 to train Javelin FAW.9 crews for the Far East and Cyprus. Here it was again training Phantom crews initially in attack and reconnaissance, moving to all-weather fighter training in 1973. Training stopped when the Spey engine turbines started to crack, then there was a further delay when the OCU deployed to Cyprus during the Turkish invasion of the north.

No. 228 OCU this time for me meant the back seat of the Phantom and a very different sort of organisation. There were two distinct phases of training, basic and advanced, and an all-important ground school and simulator unit. The QFIs and the basic navigators converted student crews to the Phantom, then the weapons instructors taught them the weapons system and air-combat manoeuvring. There was a fair amount of crossover, but the distinction was essential. However, it was still strange being back, having to wear an immersion (dry) flying suit and flying almost exclusively over the North Sea. RAF Coningsby meant married quarters, the village school and the rather lovely countryside once we became used to it.

The RAF Phantoms' back seats were not designed for a pilot. For a navigator, the radar and controls would be pulled out after take-off. With the rear control column fitted they were wire-locked forward. Visibility forwards was problematic and the high angle of attacks were shown by small lights called indexers. You got used to it though as there was no choice. A staff navigator explained the workings of INAS, and the well-kept secret of using the lines of tar on the apron for rapid heading alignments. Reverse crew rides in the simulator gradually made sense of the handling of the radar for air intercepts. The all-important thing to remember was that a radar contact weighed 20 tons and deserved significant respect.

On my first staff meeting, the boss had a draw for who would fly the spare aircraft for the Phantom aerobatic pilot to his various show venues. I guess I won that with the only overseas show at Aviano, a USAF base in northern Italy. All weekends away were fantastic breaks from teaching but this was the clear winner. In the event we flew two clean (that is to say no external fuel tanks) to RAF Wildenrath to refuel. Then by some sleight of hand we had clearance to overfly Austria on a direct heading to Aviano. The American hospitality was lavish, they loved the Phantom aerobatic

The author with his son James and wife Wendy at home in 1981 photographed for the *Lincolnshire Echo* after the announcement of being awarded the Queen's Commendation for Valuable Service in the air.

show and Monday morning was a total anti-climax. Indeed, French air traffic control was once again on strike, so that the RAF Jaguars and the Canadian F-104s based in Germany were stuck. We made a half plan for one of us to take the Jaguars and the other the F-104s in close formation to make just two radar contacts over Austria, but the Americans stopped it as soon as they realised what was about to happen.

The students were in the main straight from training and were mostly of a very high standard. The occasional upgrading Vulcan captain was more of a challenge, but they all got through in the end. I was made station flight safety officer (SFSO) quite early on then got promoted and awarded the Queen's Commendation for Valuable Service in the Air, I guess for my time spent in Germany. What a mouthful. The downside was that this would inevitably mean an early posting, which happened at the start of the following year. In the meantime we came together as a reserve squadron, 64(R), for national exercises, and we managed to fit in two weeks each firing the gun in Cyprus.

As SFSO I flew with the director of Flight Safety, an air commodore, who wanted to see why a Phantom was hard to fly at high angles, and how a departure took place (autorotation and spinning). He saw how fuel dumped at high angle would circulate forward over the wing's leading edge, and then had a try at flying at an approach angle just using the indexers. Any aileron input would make the aircraft depart so directional control was through the rudder pedals. Needless to say, he managed to depart from normal flight into a series of flick rolls. "Do you know what's happened Sir?" FLICK "I take it that this is a Phantom departure." "Yes Sir, can you remember the recovery?" "No, I don't think I can." FLICK "Would you like me to take control and show you?" FLICK "I would be awfully grateful if you would." "I HAVE CONTROL." He was seriously cool.

The Air Officer Commanding 11 Group designate took me through Mach 1 with afterburner selected at 10,000 feet pointing vertically downwards, muttering about his stomach valve. I called him a very rude name concerning his birth status, and jiggled out the afterburners. He recovered the aircraft by 2,000 feet. Phew! "Young man, nobody has called me that in at least 20 years. However, in the circumstances I consider it somewhat appropriate. Shall we return to the fight?" I had inserted the position into the INAS. Then I took him back into the fight to claim shots on the two other Phantoms we were training with. He was euphoric. An instructor should never take control too early, and that's eventually what got me posted to the Tactical Leadership Programme, two years later.

Then on another occasion on a student's first flight ever in a Phantom the flaps broke with a loud bang as we joined the circuit. I gradually realised the awful truth that I would have to land flapless from the back seat and hand back control on the ground. Forward visibility was zero, and the approach speed was almost 200 knots, something that staff instructors practised together occasionally but never took very seriously until it actually happened. It involved a Spitfire-style turning approach rolling out at 200 feet and hoping to see the runway over the student's shoulder. The station commander wrote: "The instructor did his job. Well."

So that was that. I had qualified once again as an instrument rating examiner, renewed my A2 Instructor rating on the Phantom, then, after a short holiday in Greece, we were off to RAF Leuchars where I was posted as squadron QFI (training officer) to 111 Squadron, and back into maritime air defence. You rarely get any choice in the matter. I secretly wanted to stay at Coningsby in dear old Lincolnshire with a chance to fly the actual Spitfire.

111(F) SQUADRON, RAF LEUCHARS, 1981

On my first day in Treble One Squadron there was a fuss concerning a QRA aircraft. It was short of fuel but it was on recovery, or something like that. Then out of the gloom a Phantom landed with totally clean wings. Its AIM-9G Sidewinder missiles had gone as well as the three external fuel tanks. The pilot was a youngster on his first tour, flying with a rather more experienced navigator. The story started to unfold. There was a large bit of the northern North Sea where whichever way you pointed the aircraft there was no land visible. The maximum range of the radar in mapping mode was 200 nautical miles, so if you flew a circle with no land in sight then you knew roughly where you were. In this case they didn't think they needed to as they were working with US Navy E-2 Hawkeyes since the USAF E-3 Sentry (AWACS) aircraft had been transferred to Europe at the time of the Polish shipyard riots. The US Navy had been passing them a position several hundred miles out, and they did not think they needed to check. (Moral there somewhere.)

When it was time to go home, they made the 360-degree sweep and hearts sank as there was no land visible in the radar, neither the Shetlands, the Faroes, Norway nor Iceland. The nav advised that if they cleaned off the aircraft to reduce aerodynamic drag, they could just make Iceland with empty tanks. We heard afterwards that once the situation was widely understood, the USAF KC-130 Tanker crew, assigned to their search and rescue helicopter, ran for their aircraft with a "We'll get him". We never discovered whether this could have been achieved, because at the Sector Operations Centre at RAF Buchan near Aberdeen, the split in responsibilities to Europe and

North America became apparent. "What's the problem?" came the question from the US side of the situation map. "We've a Phantom running out of fuel trying to make Iceland." "Oh, can we offer you our tanker?" An RAF Victor of course.

Within the first month I was on Northern QRA when I was scrambled off to fire a missile at RAF Valley. A Jindivik target drone was airborne from Llanbedr, a Lightning was waiting at Bardsey Island to provide photo chase and the firing of an AIM-9G Sidewinder went off perfectly. The drone escaped again by releasing a towed flare for the missile to follow, fuse against and explode. Its munition at the time was a set of metal rods which would expand and chop a target aircraft into pieces, later proved when a Germany Phantom accidentally fired on a Jaguar and chopped the aircraft in half. After this firing we landed at RAF Valley for the missile people to check the missile pylons, before flying back to Leuchars and what remained of a day in the QRA shed and more television.

Leuchars lies in a most beautiful part of Scotland at the eastern side of Perthshire and in sight of St Andrews. At the west end there is Lucklaw Hill, where my grandfather was raised. In fact, the bush telegraph moved quickly to report that one of the family had come back, and the locals took a great interest in our affairs. The local school was initially excellent, but life in married quarters there could be stressful. A flood the following winter didn't help, followed by a fire in the house next door into which we moved. I actually loved the place but it was difficult for the family. The flying was wonderful with hundreds of miles of land and sea over which to train, even the Haar which descends on Leuchars as the ice melts in the hills. I have actually landed at the west end of the runway and gone into thick fog before turning off at the other end.

Treble One Squadron had a comparatively unusual history, formed as a part of the Royal Flying Corps in Palestine in 1917. They suffered a short disbandment thereafter but reformed in time for the Battle of Britain with distinguished service around Dunkirk. The squadron diary records that in 1937 (squadron at Northolt) an uncle of one of the pilots was the Chester Herald of the College of Arms. He apparently remarked that the RAF was still using the mishmash of identifying badges from the First World War, and set out to design something better. He came up with what is now the default badge, in this case incorporating the scimitars from the Middle East, the Cross of Jerusalem, and the broad swords from the City of London. The RAF Board was apparently delighted and this became the RAF's unit badge design up to the present day. When equipped with the Hawker Hunter the squadron provided the aerobatic team 'The Black Arrows', famous for its 22-aircraft loop (with a little help from its friends), and after the Phantom and Tornado F.3, finally sadly disbanded in 2011.

The flying was invariably challenging, despite having to spend a lot of time in the back seat. My predecessor had been mostly occupied doing 'vital' squadron work other than training and standards and there was a lot of catching up to be done. After the missile came a session of dissimilar air combat training (DACT) with the USAF Aggressor Squadron's F-5Es, based at RAF Alconbury. The two pilots kept explaining that they were simulators, but our own level of air combat training was almost non-existent and we wanted instruction. It was a good week though.

The F-5E is the sports version of the Northrop F-5A light fighter, in which I later flew quite often. The F-5A is in fact a rather pedantic but vice-free high-performance aircraft, nowhere near as responsive as, say, a Hawk, but capable. Its self defence capability is slight but it has sold all over the world. The F-5E puts this right with an excellent turning performance if lacking a little in power. Once Phantom energy management was understood, they were not hard to beat. The Americans loved them since they simulated most closely the subsonic MiGs from Vietnam. Generals always like to train for the last war, but of course new aggressor aircraft replaced the F-5Es some years ago. (The Czech L-39 is fast becoming the go-to aggressor aircraft.) We were lucky to have the chance to work with them despite the disaster of taking the pilots to the first-generation curry house in St Andrews. Haggis Pakora was a long way in the future.

I should add that our aircraft was the F-4K, or RAF FG.1, as was our partner squadron's, 43. This particular muddle went back to the cancellation of a sister aircraft carrier to HMS *Ark Royal.* There were various changes to make it suitable for carrier work, for example an extending nose leg for carrier take-offs, a slot on the stabiliser leading edge for better landing control, and traffic lights on the nosewheel door for the ship's landing safety officer to monitor an approaching aircraft's angle of attack. There was no battery and the navigation system was a joke. In fact, the FG.1's back cockpit was described as an ergonomic slum full of exposed plumbing. The wing fold was a delight, which the RAF disabled as soon as they could. A converting pilot got used to the differences very quickly.

Leuchars had a secondary runway, all of 4,500 feet, which the Chipmunks used. At some point the navy had equipped it with a purpose use arrestor gear (PUAG), so that a Phantom might land on the short runway if the main runway was blocked and allow pilots initial and continuity experience of landing into a cable. The station commander invited me to try it out, and it worked brilliantly, even at night.

Once the Phantom had come to rest with a jolt somewhere between a more usual runway cable and an aircraft carrier, there was enough elasticity to pull the aircraft back. The cable dropped away from the hook, and the pilot could then retract the hook and taxi clear. The duty fireman had an oil temperature gauge which told him whether to apply the cooling pump while the cable was pulled back ready for the next aircraft. A PUAG engagement became an essential part of a new pilot's joining programme at Leuchars, and it allowed us to use the hook from time to time for landings on the short runway.

Then in June we had a short gunnery session over the North Sea, and in August I was off to the German air base at Jever in Lower Saxony to take part in the Tactical Leadership Programme TLP2 7/81 for a month. That meant nothing at the time, but it would be a life changer. I was crewed with Paul Pike, call sign Frog, and we were to go with a crew from 43 Squadron. We had no idea how to get there, so I called the Devon crew at Edinburgh Castle. The admiral there had an RAF Devon aircraft at his beck and call, and the conversation went something like: "Will the admiral be using his barge on this particular date?" "No, nothing in the book." "Well, he doesn't want it that day so can we have it?" "You cheeky sods, but I don't see why not." And that was how we loaded up the boxes of duty-free, kissed the families goodbye, and set off for Germany on a fine Sunday morning. The aircraft and our ground crew would follow a week later.

TLP2 7/81, GERMAN AIR FORCE JULY 1981

Jever air base on a damp Sunday evening was deserted, and the Devon crew went straight off to a hotel. Our rooms were fairly primitive by RAF standards and the German air force (GAF) had left an intelligence test which we all failed, namely a do-it-yourself duvet made by inserting blankets inside a sheet. The *Offizierheim* was unwelcoming that evening, but we gradually met the other participants who had arrived by road and were as underwhelmed as we were. However, the building was a magnificent example of German design. It even boasted a minstrels' gallery in the grand dining room which the RAF had blocked up in the 1950s to stop young aircrew jumping off onto arm chairs. (It was an RAF fighter base until the Sandys axe.) Jever airfield, situated near the North Sea coast of Lower Saxony, had itself been a vital air-defence airfield in the Second World War sitting as it did on the American B-17s' route to Berlin. It now housed the GAF's OTU 10, where pilots were converted onto the F-104 Starfighter after flying training in the USA. The commander was a former

Second World War fighter pilot, Oberst Hans Klaffenbach, reputed to heartily dislike the RAF. That was day one.

The Tactical Leadership Programme was an idea that had come in the mid-1970s for NATO air crews to get together, train together and form mutual understanding and trust. As any possible Central Region conflict would involve a disparate mixture of air forces, with small but more effective numbers, working together was becoming vital. With this aim in mind, in January 1978, the signatory nations Belgium, Canada, Germany, the Netherlands, the UK and the USA formed the Allied Air Forces Central Europe TLP at the German air force base of Fürstenfeldbruck, just north of Munich. Early TLP courses took the form of a two-week seminar where aircrew discussed and formulated NATO tactics, techniques and procedures. This training was ground school only and accordingly in September 1979 TLP moved to Jever to commence flying, and in the nine years at Jever, 71 courses took place and 2,000 NATO aircrew graduated. In the end aircraft noise complaints won, as well as the GAF wanting the TLP hangars and accommodation for a second Tornado squadron as the F-104s were replaced.

In all NATO units the boss is invariably from the host nation. At Jever this was Dirk Weimer, who was that rare combination of fighter pilot and politician with perfect English. We met our fellow participants and the TLP staff, and discovered a mix of officers and NCOs from the participating nations. For our four-week course, No. 7 of 1981, we had a Norwegian pair from Rygge, by invitation, flying silver-

German air force F-104s.

painted F-5As in air defence, as well as a German pair from Hopsten flying F-4Fs for whom air defence was a secondary role. In fact, they didn't like the role that much and, like most bomber pilots, really did not attempt to understand it. The 12 air-to-ground crews were four USAF F-111s from Lakenheath in the UK, two USAF F-4Gs 'Wild Weasels' from Spangdahlem in the Moselle Valley, two GAF F-104s, two Dutch F-5As (painted green and brown) and two RAF Buccaneers from RAF Laarbruch. This was classified as a long-range course that could roam greater distances from Jever.

The first week was ground school, and we staggered through the first day when the GAF pilots explained how we should have made up the duvets. At five o'clock we went in flying suits to the bar in the officers' mess, where there was a 'happy hour' every day. At about ten o'clock, Oberst Klaffenbach came into the bar with his Group staff, and started to play a German dice game with intervals involving a foul schnapps called *Weisser Tod* (White Death). Our TLP boss pointed him out with a health warning for RAF officers. It just made no sense, so I went and stood at the Oberst's shoulder and waited until he turned round with a "Yes?" I reported: "British detachment, privilege to be here, any problems etc., etc." Klaffy stared at me trying to detect cynicism. There was none. "Ordnance, Runde Weissentodt". And I was on his team until the day he retired. The boss asked me how I knew the way that a commander should be approached in the pre-war Luftwaffe. I didn't. It just seemed obvious. On that evening though, I didn't know that I would be back.

At the weekend our aircraft and ground crew arrived from Leuchars. We took two of the Americans to Wildenrath for the weekend in their minibus, and then on the Monday the flying started, fairy gently at first. Our brains were full of weapons and tactics, especially those of the other course participants, and then we started to work against them, trying out all sorts of air-defence scenarios, while the 12 air-to-ground aircraft flew every kind of attack mission imaginable. Our radars failed on a regular basis so our results were pretty unimpressive. The squadron at Leuchars was increasingly fed up with sending out replacement aircraft. Things did look up towards the end though, but we lost a lot of credibility as a new weapon system with a 'look-down shoot-down' capability. As many weapons systems as possible were introduced including the E-3A Sentry, at the time a USAF facility, plus American and German fighter control. An A-10 Thunderbolt was even flown in so that we could be briefed on it.

Jever town was a perfect jewel and the East Frisians were friendly and welcoming. We went to Spangdahlem with the Americans for one weekend and for the other I hitched a ride to Leeuwarden in a Dutch air force Alouette 3 helicopter with a Dutch female pilot, unique at the time, who had been providing forward air control. It was a strange aircraft to fly with a live cyclic control column that you could not release for a second, although the throttle was automatic. Suddenly the course was coming to an end. The Americans obliged by sending over two F-5E Aggressor aircraft to act as enemy air while all 18 participating aircraft flew together for the last two missions. I escorted the F-111s and ended up with a close range shot on one of the F-5s, and then nearly ran myself out of fuel as the sea fog rolled in and Jever went to radar approaches. We were number 17 in the queue. Neighbouring Wittmundhafen was no better where we were number nine in the Wittmund queue, so I took a deep breath and recovered fast and low ahead of the radar stream. Air traffic control was not amused. It was not a great piece of flying.

Oberst Klaffenbach sent for me, and the boss predicted disaster. Klaffy instead gathered Group staff into his office and broke out bottles of Jever Pils. "Al, I hear you did a great piece of flying today. Well done." I presented him with a Leuchars plaque and we all went off to the officers' mess to hang it on the wall. He told me about flying the Spitfire on a specialist unit that demonstrated captured aircraft. Apparently, they were painted white underneath so that the German gunners could recognise them. "Did it work?" I asked. "No, I was shot down three times." He had never had the slightest interest in politics, so this was the man that represented the old Luftwaffe for its new pilots. Klaffy stayed on for the end-of-course party and made a speech saying how welcome we all were. The boss shook his head in amazement. And that was that. We flew back the next day, my tactical call sign 'Banjo' firmly established and for a while I had never felt so sharp. I just wondered if there might be any possibility of getting the RAF's slot on the air defence staff there.

Dan and George, our two American friends came over to Leuchars from Spangdahlem on the Moselle, in a pair of F-4G Phantom Wild Weasels with their squadron boss, Gerry Lyn. They stayed for the summer ball and I flew illegally with Gerry in the F-4G the next day. The aircraft was a modified F-4E and was optimised for its Shrike anti-radiation missile to attack radars, or bomb them, so at its heart was a device to triangulate radar emissions, and I even managed to lock in the fighter control station at Boulmer. However, Gerry explained afterwards that it would be best to keep quiet about it as the system was strictly 'NOFORN'[9] but I had kindly flown to help Dan out with a possible hangover. The next year Gerry and Dan flew into the Moselle banks in poor visibility, with fatal results; two more good friends down.

[9] NOFORN simply meant 'No foreigners allowed'.

During the remainder of 1981, we had a week's detachment at Machrihanish near the Mull of Kintyre, and had a wonderful time flying around the Hebrides in gloriously free airspace. In early 1982, the squadron deployed to Decimomannu, where an instrumented sea range allowed accurate replay of air combat scenarios, especially against the USAF F-15s. A low-level cross-country flight in an RAF Jaguar T.2 was a bonus event hugging the rugged scenery.

Then in the spring of 1982, I managed to get seats on an RAF VC10 to take the family to the USA spending time around Washington DC and in Florida and Disneyworld. Just as we were leaving Dulles to fly home, I picked up a copy of *Newsweek* with a picture of HMS *Hermes* on the cover with the two-inch banner 'THE EMPIRE STRIKES BACK'. The Falklands campaign had started.

THE FALKLANDS CAMPAIGN – THE HOME FRONT

In the spring of 1982, the navy and the army went to war. Massive efforts were then made to involve the RAF, culminating in the deployment of the entire tanker force to Ascension Island, the onward deployment of 1 Squadron's Harriers to join the navy on the two South Atlantic aircraft carriers, the planned deployment of Chinook heavy-lift helicopters and Operation Black Buck, when a Vulcan put a bomb on the Stanley runway, and repeated the operation several times against Argentinian radars. And, of course, the RAF's transports were working non-stop. All servicemen want to go into action, and it is particularly frustrating to see others getting involved from the touchline. Eventually, when it seemed that we were winning, the army engineers promised that as soon as Stanley airfield was taken, they would have a short runway available with an arrestor wire at the mid-point. This would include 1,500 feet of PSP (pierced steel planking) runway which had vanished from an airfield in Florida. The Americans were quietly supplying massive support in less obvious ways.

The station commander asked me to find out how short a distance was needed to land a Phantom, no questions asked. The answer was that by streaming the brake parachute at about 200 feet rather than after landing, and by touching down at 21 units angle of attack instead of the usual 19, an FG.1 might be stopped in 2,000 feet or 2,500 feet if the runway was wet. The FGR.2 might be just a little longer, but it was not easy. Certainly, by using this technique at Stanley you would know whether landing was going to be a problem. A plan came together to have eight FGR.2s ready to deploy to Ascension and thence to Stanley, in the event that the Argentinians

Air-to-air refuelling with a USAF KC-135.

carried on the conflict from the mainland. Sixteen crews including myself were put on standby with a bag packed in the spare room.

Squadron training did change just a bit. The Victor tankers had all vanished and we started to train with the USAF KC-135s. This is essentially a boom-operated system where an operator behind a backwards-facing window steers an extending nozzle to make contact with a trap built into the receiving aircraft. However, the US Navy uses the highly flexible method of attaching a pod to a carrier aircraft, then usually an A-6 Intruder, (now an /3-18 and in the near future a drone tanker), to stream a flexible hose. The refuelling aircraft than flies its probe into the basket. Both methods achieved amazing results in the Vietnam war and some fighters, for example the F-105 Thunderchief, were even equipped with both systems. The KC-135s all carried a 13-foot semi-flexible metal hose which had to be attached to the boom prior to take-off to service 'probe and drogue' refuelling.

To receive fuel from a KC-135, it was necessary not just to fly the probe into the basket but then fly a kink into the hose to open a mechanical valve. Extraction required the reverse and the coupling was merciless in snapping off a probe if it was done wrong. More often than not the KCs came from RAF Mildenhall where the smiling boom operator was wearing a farmer's cloth cap and invariably tried to help by steering the basket towards the probe. They were on a separate radio frequency, had lots of banter and were amusing if a little frustrating. Later modified Vulcans started to appear with a single centreline hose; a great addition to the tanker fleet which lasted for a number of years.

The Nimrod fleet had been assured years before that they would always operate within air supremacy. This would clearly not now be the case, so on a Saturday morning we took two Phantoms to RAF Kinloss to introduce them to the fighter world. Before leaving we grabbed Airfix 1:72 scale models of both the Phantom and the Mirage III. The Nimrod crews were assembled in a hangar and I paced out 1:72 of the distance that an air-to-air missile might be fired. They just did not believe that the fighter looked that small. We moved onto guns range which terrified them. Then we flew three sorties against a Nimrod packed with spectators, including head-on guns engagements. "Why would you want to do that?" "To kill the pilots." "Oh!"

Well, the Nimrod was quickly modified to carry its own air-to-air missiles. The operators became very slick at countermeasures and three weeks later they were able to fight back. It was impressive. We took a pair of Phantoms to help them learn air-to-air refuelling for which there were still available Victors. I spent an hour flying alongside explaining the noble art over the radio and in no time, they were competent at air-to-air refuelling also. There were more far-fetched ideas of re-equipping our FG.1s for carrier work to fly off an American carrier; probably just as well that this came to nothing. However, we did spend time on the Tain range on the Dornoch Firth, learning how to shoot the Gatling against ground targets until we were getting quite reasonable scores.

Months before the Falklands though, someone had the very bright idea to twin each air-defence Phantom squadron with a Royal Navy Type-42 destroyer, the navy's air defence. Treble One Squadron drew HMS *Southampton,* a brand-new ship at the start of its work up. The ship spent a few days in Leith where I was able to plan their participation in a large-scale exercise with the first lieutenant, and during his

Nimrod air-to-air refuelling over the North Sea.

subsequent tour of the ship, he pointed out all the weaknesses in the ship's defences and ability to survive an engagement. Every word was borne out when HMS *Sheffield*, a sister ship, was struck by an Argentinian Exocet missile and sank. They were incredibly grateful to be involved in a large-scale exercise where their defensive systems could be exercised. They invited the squadron to a memorable evening cocktail party where the boss insisted on calling their captain 'Brian'.

When the ship was due to be commissioned, in Southampton water of course, we took four Phantoms to RNAS Yeovilton overnight then flew a low-level flypast for them the next morning. The marine bandmaster switched straight into 'Those Magnificent Men'. Then the Southampton air traffic controller said, "Hey, don't forget us". We duly obliged with a four-aircraft attack on Southampton Airport. As the time for them to deploy to the South Atlantic approached we hosted a party for them at Leuchars. They all wore name tags and were all called Brian. The boss never realised why.

HMS *Southampton* sailed from Portsmouth on Sunday 16 May, loaded up with chaff countermeasures in every spare corner. We had taken two aircraft to Yeovilton on the Friday and had done some air-combat training with a couple of remaining Sea Harriers. We were invited on board *Southampton* for the Saturday and were flown off in their Lynx helicopter. Then on the Sunday as HMS *Southampton* sailed down the Channel, we flew two sorties each against them with continuous attacks simulating an Étendard first of all with the radar in search mode, then taking a lock on the ship. (The Étendard was the French naval fighter sold to the Argentinians.) We then simulated firing the Exocet missile, shut down the radar for a minute then started up again in a different mode to simulate the missile's own radar. It was the only chance they had to bring all their electronic countermeasures into play. It wasn't much, but we didn't go to the war. We had done what we could.

CYPRUS ONWARDS, AIR DISPLAYS AND EXERCISES

My opposite number on 43 Squadron was Dave Cyster, who owned two Tiger Moths and had flown a Moth to Australia and also a Dragon Rapide to Cape Town. We shared a lot of the training and standards work providing dual checks as required, flying VIPs, planning station exercises and so on. It was a good working relationship, and he let me fly his second Tiger Moth. We had space in a hangar, bought fuel from the RAF, flew off a small grass strip, and made frequent aerobatic practices over Fife. As the Leuchars Open Day approached, just after Battle of Britain Day, we were asked if we would like to fly in the air show, so the hard work started off with finding out who had the finer pitch propeller, therefore who should fly in which slot. Dave would thus lead in the Australia aircraft, which only he flew, and I would find out very quickly how to fly on the wing. He also had a radio. This led quickly to a pairs take-off and a climb in close formation to 500 feet, mainly in line abreast formation because it looks difficult. In fact, sitting behind the wing, it is quite easy to maintain.

We would then dive at the crowd, split to opposite ends of the runway, looping on the way, a stall turn at the extremity, then a neat formation re-join and a pairs landing. Overconfident? Probably. The next evolution was to tie the wings together with pretty ribbon from the seamstress in the village. By cutting a small nick in the ribbon's halfway point we ensured that on the split we had even amounts of ribbon matched to another ribbon on the other wing. Hendon Air Display? Easy. We guessed a crosswind limitation of 15 knots, discovered that my civil licence was out of date and quickly arranged a check flight with the Dundee flying club on the morning of the air day with their ex-RAF CFI.

The Tiger Moth pair at RAF Leuchars air display with Dave Cysters flying on the left and the author flying on the right.

Flying a Phantom at RAF Akrotiri Open Day.

Then on the day, of course, the crosswind was 17 knots. We drove all over Leuchars in the air traffic Land Rover looking for an into-wind stretch of grass, but there was nowhere devoid of rocks or barbed wire. "Your call Al." "Lets' do it." And I shall never forget watching the ribbon gradually stretching out, Dave's head going back, then on his nod we snatched the aircraft off the ground just enough to close the gap. We got a ripple of applause from the squadron and 50,000 spectators never noticed that the ribbon was about to break. Phew! A year later I gave the second air display in a Phantom for the Akrotiri Open Day, and was censured for the short landing which we had developed for the short runway at Stanley.

The Swedes visited in September 1982, two lieutenant colonels and a one-star general. I was given the task of flying them in a chase aircraft when we were due to fire the Skyflash air-to-air missile in trial. They needed to be briefed, taken into the simulator, suitably equipped and entertained for a few days, flying the two lieutenant colonels on successive firings. The engagement would be in a Hebrides range, against a drone fired from a Canberra 70 nautical miles down range, which would immediately climb to 70,000 ft. The firing aircraft needed to be supersonic at around 25,000 feet, and the missile would accelerate and take out the height difference. This then needed a Victor tanker, a Phantom designated as the primary firer, a secondary firer should the primary aircraft fail at the last moment and an airborne spare. I would tag on the end with my Swede and make sure he could see the firing. The Brits were as anxious to sell Skyflash to Sweden as the Swedes were to buy it. It would equip their J37 Viggen air-defence fighter. All very exciting.

It all went as advertised. The Swedes drank me dry and entertained with Swedish drinking ditties that all seemed to end in "OY". On the flying days everyone was serviceable and the join with the tanker worked perfectly at the western end of the firing range over Benbecula. The missile was a joy to watch as it disappeared upwards and everyone was happy. On my second chase I was with Åke Lindqvist, who ran the Saab J37 Viggen development flight at Norrköping, south-west of Stockholm. After the firing I took him to Benbecula airfield, where the fighter controllers with whom we had just been working, all came out to wave. When we got back to Leuchars their light aircraft transport was waiting and it was a rushed goodbye. The Swedes bought Skyflash and a year later I made a staff visit to Norrköping. Åke remained a good friend until he sadly died of cancer some years later.

Cyprus came round again later in the month, when we would deploy in three waves of four aircraft two hours apart. We would top up from a Vulcan tanker off the Suffolk coast, and enter French airways opposite the Isle of Wight. A ground crew party had departed in the small hours to see the aircraft through Brindisi in southern Italy. What could go wrong? The boss set off first with the B Flight commander. The A Flight commander was to follow and I would bring on whoever was left. I was flying with Bob Crane, the squadron weapons instructor, and a bit of map study indicated the weak point of the plan which was that the TACAN (military distance and bearing beacon) had to be working to make an accurate arrival into France. Bob carefully worked out the radar picture of the Isle of Wight, and we briefed our section accordingly in case our radar failed as well as the TACAN. And that's exactly what happened. We joined French airways, then Italian airways and landed at Brindisi. The ground crew party had seen the first section through, but there was no sign of the second section. Lost in France?

The missing section turned up the next day. They had avoided French airways completely, and French military radar had eventually turned them back to make them start again. When they arrived in Italy, they realised they had inadequate fuel for Brindisi, and elected to land at Grazzanise, near Naples. The Italians simply did not hold vast stocks of fuel but gave them enough to get to Brindisi. They were now out of hours and RAF Akrotiri in Cyprus had in any case closed for the day. The entire party therefore awarded themselves a night out in a Brindisi hotel and continued the next day. Then the signals started to arrive, diplomatic protests from both the French and Italians, demands for explanations from HQ 11 Group, protests from Command accounts and from Air Support Command for delaying their C-130 transport. The flight leader beamed at everyone, bought a picture frame in the NAAFI and hung up the signals for all to read. I guess that's how it's done.

I flew the planned sequence in the Akrotiri Air Display at the weekend, then took off to the resident Wessex helicopter squadron to see if I could pick up some lessons. Someone else could have a go running the desk. The squadron, No. 84, had a split role of national air-sea rescue and United Nations support, moving UN troops as required and supporting the more remote observation posts on the 'Green Line' which divided Cyprus between the Turkish north and the Greek south. I was lucky in that they were about to be standardised by the Central Flying School (Helicopters), and the examiner had spare hours to become current on the Wessex. I spent a blissful week flying a totally new type of aircraft with a highly paid man who would work the radio and take care of any red lights. We spent a day in the Troodos mountain range supporting the UN's Danish battalion there, a day wet winching and a day supporting the RAF Regiment who were about to deploy to Northern Ireland. Fun though it was, I did enough helicopter flying to know that this was not for me. It was great to be back in the Phantom, and the gunnery was addictive as ever.

The month was over all too soon, including a weekend in the Turkish north, marred by a misunderstanding with Cyprus Special Branch man on return through the Green Line. Fortunately, he was a friend of Niasi, formerly a Limassol restauranteur and now a hotelier in Kyrenia where we had stayed. We then set off for home in the same manner as we had planned to arrive. This time when my section arrived in Brindisi though, the previous eight aircraft were lined up with the C-130. We had known that there was sometimes a communications problem between the Italian approach and tower control. We had checked with the tower in advance as to which runway was in use. They said south, so we duly positioned. The first section had believed approach, had joined for the north runway and had a near miss with a McDonnell Douglas DC-9. The Italian station commander had arrived to see what the problem was, and had patiently listened to the boss's views and on foreigners in general before he threw us out.

Europe was well and truly closed with autumnal poor visibility everywhere but Decimomannu would have us. We were there for four days before the Wildenrath weather cleared enough for us to stage through on a Sunday with the help of their station flight who gaped at the boss's carpet slippers, worn since he fell into the bonfire the previous evening. A few of us had overnight kit in shopping bags on the floor of the aircraft, but most had not bothered. We arrived back at Leuchars in the dark to a round of disbelieving families and squadron engineers. Soon after this I was off to Skrydstrup in Denmark to take part in their annual NATO tactical evaluation. A Dominie took me there with a night stop at RAF Finningley, and I was able to fly both legs. It was a ridiculously easy aircraft to fly. The skill was in understanding how to use it as an airliner. The Danes had just traded in their F-100s for their brand-new F-16s. I had one flight in an F-16B and saw that this was the future; it is one of the few aircraft where all you have to do is think something and the aircraft does it. I flew in F-16s many times over the next few years, without question the best aircraft I have ever flown. Flying at 9 G, like Danish air force politics, never stopped being horrible though, despite the ejection seat being raked at 30 degrees.

I took a two-aircraft detachment to Keflavik in Iceland in the January for a USAF air-defence exercise with their 57th Fighter Squadron (the Black Knights flying the F-4E Phantom). The weather was foul but the bar was free after we had paid an entry fee of a box of duty-free Glenmorangie. The Americans used an inspired madness to get them through the Icelandic winter. "Like *M*A*S*H?*" my wife asked afterwards. "Yes, just like *M*A*S*H.*" We flew once in the week, landed from a US Navy talk-down and taxied back in the next snow storm, glued to the flashing tail light of the Phantom in front. Even today, should I hear 'Bat Out of Hell' being played, I still have an impulse to get clear of the surface and be a bat. Failure meant buying everyone a round, but who cared? It was all free, and the flight surgeon ran the bar.

The Falklands War had been over since the previous June and we were facing the pretty miserable prospect of Falklands garrison duty living in tents. Either I or Dave Cyster would have to go as the training and standards officer. However, it seemed that our AOC 11 Group had intervened and arranged for me to go back to Jever in north Germany, on the staff of the Tactical Leadership Programme. My personnel officer telephoned with the news. "When do you want me to go?" I asked. "Quite soon but it seems they want you to go to Arizona first." Dave was not happy, but then later on he got a wonderful tour in India which I hope made up for it. And he was still kind enough to lend me his Australia Tiger Moth to renew my civil instructor's rating. The examiner even drove down from Perth for the occasion.

At some point we had the scramble that was the one you hope won't happen. I scrambled from QRA with Pete, a great but height-challenged nav known as 'R2-D2'. Clearly the reporting system had seen the Russians coming round the North Cape, with plenty of time to get a tanker airborne first. So, we rendezvoused with the Victor somewhere north of the Shetlands at night in high cirrus cloud with increasing

Images of the Tu-95 Bear Ds taken during QRA scramble.

air turbulence. The tanker captain decided to climb to get clear of cloud, but we never did. Then the navigator in charge of refuelling announced that the main hose drum unit, which delivered at 4,000 lbs a minute, was unserviceable, so we would tank from one of the wing pods (1,750 lbs a minute). Around 33,000 feet, it was necessary to light an afterburner then retard the other throttle to stay connected, so refuelling took a long time as fuel was consumed almost as fast as the tanker could deliver. A nightmare. It took a while to connect with the basket dancing all over the sky, and what seemed like an age to get the fuel. It was horrible.

We intercepted two Tupolev Tu-95 Bear Ds from the Soviet navy at around 17,000 feet. We had been told to get door numbers because they had been deploying aircraft from the Far East to the White Sea and intel wanted to know more. It was a pitch-black night though, so we crept forward beneath the lead aircraft so that Pete could read the door numbers through his night scope. "No good, you'll have to light an afterburner." Personally, I am right under the Bear craning my head back to hold formation. Then almost immediately: "Forget all that, just back out the way you came in." "Now look at your altimeter." We were at 3,000 feet going down fast, so I guess he was trying to wipe us off on the sea. Nice try. "Thanks, Pete." The fact was that the Soviet air force was generally friendly but Gorshkov's navy were not. Maybe they just disliked being the junior service.

My last QRA scramble was for a squadron changeover during a period when practice intercepts were prohibited in armed aircraft. We flew the two armed Phantoms over to Norway, did a couple of visual circuits at Stavanger, and came home. My last 111 Squadron flight was a six-aircraft leader's benefit over the North Sea, based on a Second World War manual of fighter tactics. Amazingly they all still worked. Germany, here I come, an essential two days to get the paperwork done and buy a car, then on to Arizona.

CHAPTER NINE

TACTICAL LEADERSHIP PROGRAMME

YUMA VISIT TO THE USMC, 1983

"Look out to the right and you'll see New York." That's not exactly what you'd expect to hear as the starboard wing drops 45 degrees. Sure enough there's the Statue of Liberty, and even the Staten Island ferry 35,000 feet below. We are in the small passenger cabin of a GAF Boeing 707, strictly teetotal, en route from Cologne to El Paso. It's a long way from Leuchars and even further from Stanley. In the last three days I have been to RAF Gütersloh to 'arrive' back in RAF Germany, bought a car from a person I met in the accounts office, driven to RAF Wildenrath and then to Wahn, the German military side of Cologne Airport. I have met five of my new colleagues from the Tactical Leadership Programme who are currently all trying to get a picture of New York. Heinz is a German F-104 pilot, the TLP operations officer, Wolf is an ex-Prussian now Bavarian F-4F air-defence back-seater, Peer is a Dutch F-5 pilot, Roger is an RAF Buccaneer back-seater and MUMU (Colonel Mullanders) is a Belgian Mirage 5 pilot, and that's just a part of the team. The previous year the US Marine Corps from the Marine Air Weapons and Tactics Squadron 1 (MAWTS-1) at Yuma had visited Jever and this was the return visit. My own inclusion was totally fortuitous.

From El Paso, TX we said goodbye to the German air force and bought economy tickets to Phoenix, AZ. Welcome to deregulation. Nobody mentioned that flights were all running an hour late, so this was actually the previous flight stopping in

Albuquerque, NM. When the wheels went down and the cabin crew tried to remove the drinks they had only just delivered, we assumed we had been hijacked. However, it was all quite normal so we had a few hours to kill before the next flight, with our bags still en route to Phoenix. We had been up overnight, were still in various uniforms, were unshaven and probably stank. When it seemed that we would not get on the last flight of the day, Wolf, who had been up for two nights, became totally Prussian and explained their various shortcomings to the airline staff in Bavarian. We got on the flight, and a bit later were reunited with our bags sitting on the pavement at Phoenix.

The weekend involved a four-hour drive to the Grand Canyon, walking to the edge and Peer saying, "Yes, it is big, isn't it? Fancy a beer?" Then another four-hour drive back. On the Sunday morning we were one again at Phoenix Airport, this time checking in at a one-girl airline flying the Saab Metro on a long route to Los Angeles with about eight stops. The same girl sold the tickets, issued boarding cards, inspected them at the gate, escorted us out to the aircraft, made sure we all strapped in and said, "Have a nice day". Once on the ground at Yuma, when we saw the first officer unloading the bags, there was a rush to make sure they took off the right ones, apparently not always the case according to the marines who were there to meet us.

On Monday morning, flying suits mandatory, we were briefed on the role of MAWTS-1 and the current weapons and tactics instructors course where all aviation elements of the marines were brought together for a small desert war, when all the classroom theory could be worked on and realised. Actually, it seemed to be an advanced version of what we were trying to do on a shoestring at Jever. The marines had even worked out how to use the targeting pod from air-combat manoeuvring instrumentation to measure simulated air-to-ground weapons accuracy. The flying evolution was worked through a series of 'shops', each one being a branch of marine aviation. We would be assigned to a different 'shop' for each 24 hours, when they would gratefully hand us on to the next 'shop'. My logbook tells me that on the Monday I flew in a marine OV-10A Bronco, so it must have been close air support.

The Bronco was an eclectic and amazing aircraft, with an ability to support marine ground forces in a number of ways. Our TLP ground liaison officer later explained that four fully equipped parachutists could jump from the back, The mission would fly with the Bronco's clam-shell back doors removed and then to drop the paras, the pilot would pull up into the vertical where they would simply fall out. My air defence colleague said quite quietly: "That ain't a jump Tom, that's a dump!" Today's mission was to check out procedures and communications, and I was able to fly the whole trip.

The Bronco was surprisingly light on the controls with excellent engine response from its pair of turbo-props. The rear seat was elevated for all round visibility. This was a surprisingly pleasant flight and a good start to the week. It is a nice aircraft to fly.

On the Tuesday we were passed to the fighter shop where there was an opportunity to fly in the F-4S, an upgraded F-4J Phantom. Flying in the back without a stick did not appeal, and I declined. Then on the Wednesday we were passed to the tanker shop. The surprise was that we had to bring a bag and were flown in a KC-130 over to Miramar near San Diego, then the home of the Top Gun programme. Being Wednesday, the officers' club was in full swing and it was rough. If Tom Cruise had started singing, he would very quickly have been parted from his trousers and pushed through a window. In fact, that infamous film scene was shot in a San Diego hotel. The main purpose of the trip was a visit to Top Gun the next day with an excellent briefing and a tour of the facilities without a female psychologist in sight.

On the Thursday I flew in the back of an OA-4 Skyhawk, which was forgettable. The mission was to attack marine helicopters with an air refuelling interlude. My marine pilot insisted that I should fly the contact but I jibbed at the state of the basket, with its spokes broken and pointing everywhere. "That's one of the good ones!" A reminder that the marines never have enough money for everything that they want to do. The OA-4 was a neat and responsive little fighter but suffered from snaking, like a Dutch roll in the horizontal plane. So, on the Friday MUMU and I went out in a giant CH-53 to evaluate whether it was possible for a helicopter to engage an attacking fighter if equipped with AIM-9L Sidewinder missiles. The aircraft was thrown all around the sky with control handed back and forth and the crewmen hanging out of the doors calling evasion. MUMU and I just hung on.

The problem here was that when we had flown in the OA-4, we had seen that this violent manoeuvring had little effect on the fighter's gun sight. And never answered was that the AIM-9L, as an air-to-air missile attached to a helicopter needed its host aircraft launch speed to work effectively. In fact, where an early AIM-9 had been incorporated into the Chaparral surface-to-air system, it needed a rocket boost to launch. In the event it never happened. We stopped after 40 minutes for a packed lunch and started up again with another fighter, but we had time to admire the massive Arizona cacti. After the second evolution, once more parked in the desert, I was offered the right seat to fly this massive helicopter back to Yuma. It was so stable it was a delight to fly, even in formation, to land and even to taxi in.

We were told that quite recently a CH-52 had knocked down an Arizona cactus, and the pilot had been charged with reckless low flying. No cactus could be more than 50 feet tall, the minimum height for low flying. His answer was to find a 70-foot cactus, land and chop it down, then take it back to the base commander as an underslung load. The base commander agreed to cancel the low-flying charge but substitute a charge of destroying a protected species.

The weekend saw a surfeit to Tex-Mex food (the marine nachos record at a sitting was at the time 72, only beaten in the state by a youngster who managed 190), a trip into San Luis Río Colorado over the border, a day out in San Diego and a cocktail party. The following week the GAF kindly diverted their Boeing 707 into Yuma for us, and we flew back to Cologne via Dulles Airport. I seem to remember catching up with sleep at Wildenrath then driving the 400 km north to Jever. It had to be the best start to a tour ever.

YOU FIGHT LIKE YOU TRAIN. JEVER, 1983

Amazingly, just outside the Jever gates there was a small two-bedroom RAF officers' mess and a number of married quarters, retained after the RAF left Jever in the 1950s. The regional NATO air battle control centre (my words) was Sector Operations Centre No. 1 about 20 miles away at Brockzetel (near Aurich) complete with a fighter control station. The commander was an RAF air commodore (one star) and a number of the sector controllers were RAF officers, mostly ex-aircrew. A number of non-commissioned officers supported them so of course the RAF TLP staff were immediately a part of this small community. The RAF officers' mess was run by two stalwart German ladies, wives of GAF senior NCOs, whose rule was absolute. The Royal Engineers postal branch brought the mail and the duty-free petrol coupons three times a week. So, I moved in along with the American air defence staffer who was on his way home. Bubba taught me all about my new situation.

I have described my own course in 1981 in a previous chapter, along with a short description of TLP's beginnings. We had no idea at the time that after Jever, TLP would move to Florennes in Belgium into the magnificent installation built for the cruise missile programme. They were there for 20 years with the French joining the programme. Noise was ever a problem, so courses were run in France, Scotland and Italy. TLP4 then moved on to Albacete in south-east Spain under a vastly different international agreement, involving the Spanish plus the Turkish, Italians and Greeks, concentrating on asymmetric warfare, with a number of constituent ground programmes. For us though, it was a continuous amateur night with poor funding and an eye on survival of the programme itself as the noise problem got worse. In particular the RAF had uniquely failed to staff our participation beyond administrative support, with no provision for our own flying (a TLP requirement) or any kind of personnel reporting system. Our first discernible senior RAF officer was an air marshal at Ramstein, whose staff were occasionally responsible for our activities. There was no policy, no orders or instructions and our guiding document was the minutes of our staff meetings, a unique form of military common law.

The RAF contingent then consisted of a ground-attack pilot, a bomber navigator and an air-defence pilot (myself) supported by an admin clerk, an ops clerk and a ground equipment NCO, all three of them working well beyond any previous experience. In fact, the various jobs for this eclectic unit had been well thought out as to which nation provided what, and the Germans also provided a pivotal civilian driver who knew everyone at Jever, and a couple of odd-job conscripts. The working language was English but when a telephone rang the nearest person was obliged to answer and then yell out the required language. We managed most of them but were eventually beaten by Portuguese. Courses were divided into short, medium and long range and aircraft types assigned accordingly. Lightnings and Harriers, for example, could only attend short courses, while the Phantom and F-15 might attend any of them. There were eight courses a year and we were expected to do our own flying between courses as well as take leave, make any visits and complete course admin. Typing was all DIY on massive German typewriters that had the German extra characters. I went to German stores, drew a complete set of German flying equipment including their lovely grey leather flying jacket that I eventually bought from them.

Then the Belgians called from 349 Squadron at Beauvechain, my old friends from Wildenrath days. "Hey Al, we hear you're back. We have a big 35th anniversary weekend so we send the Fouga for you." This delightful but tiny Fouga Magister duly arrived on the Friday afternoon and we were off. "There are two extra checks," my pilot explained. "First, on take-off, you recheck the engines because you cannot believe that the acceleration is so slow with two engines running and before landing you recheck the gear. You cannot believe that you are still flying this close to the runway unless the gear is still up." He was right on both counts. It was a great weekend and I was rescued by MUMU and his wife for the long drive back to Jever. I slept the whole way.

We always tried to arrange visits by senior officers to coincide with courses so that course members could see that we were appreciated. If no visit was planned, then the Sector Operations Centre No. 1 commander would turn up in his flying suit and always went down well (the same senior officer who tried to spin a Phantom a few years previously when he ran RAF Flight Safety). On one occasion we invited the US Army commander of the base at Bremerhaven, who was always photographed with a baseball bat. He duly chatted to the course smacking his bat against his hand, then "Any questions?" A USAF F-15 pilot asked, "General, when I'm a general will I get a big stick like that?" The course loved it. The general had no answer.

In my first few weeks at TLP, a USAF general had visited and I had managed to scrounge a ride in his T-39 Sabreliner to give me a long weekend home at Leuchars. The pilot made a fuss about the correct paperwork and the general overruled him. So, stepping out at Lakenheath in Suffolk the look on the faces of the F-111 crews who I knew from my own TLP course were a picture. However, they got me on the night sleeper to Leuchars for an unexpected weekend off. We had decided not to move until the end of the school term so that our son could start afresh with the German school year. On the Sunday night it was back onto the sleeper and a morning flight out from RAF Northolt in an RAF Devon that was collecting delivery crews.

My first course came and went. I tried Bubba's suggestion of attempting to put together what actually took place when the fighters met the bombers, what we called the 'merge', and it was massively unsuccessful. We needed whole new debriefing techniques including 100 per cent debriefing of gunsight films with the entire air-defence team working on the problem including the American photo technician who had to develop all the films and reload all the different cameras. We had to learn how to debrief the video cassettes in use in the USAF F-15s, F-16s and A-10s. However, Bubba was right in that you could not draw any conclusions or give any advice unless it became fairly clear what really happened in the merge. It was also apparent that we were inventing scenarios instead of using the various procedures described in the Central Region standard operating procedures. So, my flight in the Dutch F-5B came as welcome relief, a nice little aircraft, more a bomber than a fighter with fairly heavy controls but a competent light-attack aircraft. Its defensive weaponry was two cannons with the electronic countermeasures, and even the Dutch were starting to lose interest in it when their F-16s started to arrive.

Then it was time to go to Wildenrath and relearn how to fly the Phantom as a junior and not receive a warm welcome as a visiting pilot. As far as the Wildenrath pilots were concerned, I was stealing their flying as none was allocated for TLP staff. This never really changed except when I turned up regularly to fly in Wildenrath exercises. After a while I started to fly with 92 Squadron for training and 19 Squadron for exercises just to split the commitment, but it was always difficult, especially maintaining a 30-day currency. It was not always possible so that meant the simulator (at RAF Brüggen) and a dual check, plus the additional requirements for maintaining an instrument rating. Later we managed to persuade the suppliers at RAF Germany to give us a staff car, shopping at the NAAFI was a must. I gradually got accredited to RAF Germany's intelligence division, but that was all in the future. In fact, to our amazement, we had a call to say that we were being issued with a brand-new staff car, which I was to collect from Brüggen, but at the end of the week to take to Gütersloh who would maintain it. I managed to hitch a ride in an RAF Chinook from the airstrip at Wegberg, which the Gütersloh Motor Transport depot refused to believe. They changed the speedometer because the delivery trip was then 165 km short.

For now, at the end of the week there was a trooper flight back to Luton, the sleeper train to Leuchars and this time a trip out with the family to Jever on North Sea Ferries. I was taking over a brand-new house that RAF Gütersloh (our parent unit) had taken on as a hiring in a village near Jever. The local headmaster of the primary school was an old-school party member who hated the British, and made every objection to James attending his school. In the end he retired and the new head welcomed James as a pupil. In the meantime, a place was found for him at the US Department of Defense army school near Jever where he spent a delightful year learning about Columbus and the Red Indians. It was a happy school though and he loved it.

There was clearly a massive amount of work to be done at Jever. In the future we were able to expand the TLP course debriefs, we brought in the fighter controllers from northern Germany, we were able to introduce participation of a NATO AWACS controller to each course (they had after all coined the term 'Iron Gorilla' to describe the TLP mission on a radar screen), solve the problem of mixed weapons systems and control at low level and define a fit-for-purpose set of air-defence tactics, which I hear were still in use at the time of the first Gulf War. We would introduce a pair of reconnaissance aircraft on six courses a year, along with a recce staff member. We would ensure that there was realistic opposition for the last two flights on each course so that sometimes we might have up to 30 aircraft airborne. Our intelligence brief was in the future which we delivered at a number of bases including the Canadians at Bad Solingen and to the Air National Guard in Arizona. "Bullshit. You fight like you train?" This mantra was sewn into a flag in the entrance hall, and very much summed up what we were trying to do. The enormity of the task was just starting to be apparent.

LIFE IN EAST FRIESLAND, WEST GERMANY'S NORTH COAST

The demands did not ease at all in the time between courses. I had started a small-scale wine club for the TLP staff to have their own label Moselle wine, totally copied from 19 Squadron. At the same time the NCOs were running a sort of convenience store for beer mugs and flying-suit patches. There was a problem and it came to a sudden halt. "You understand all this business stuff," said my German boss who had succeeded Dirk Weimer. "Go over and see what the problem is." The problem was quite simply debts of 6,000 DM and 4,500 DM of unsellable stock. "Sort it out, would you?" "*Ja, mein Colonel.*" So, we did, starting with a sale, then a shares issue, and then ventures into new lines of T-shirts, caps, key rings etc., and of course the wine. It was a lot of work, but suddenly the turnover was 250,000 DM. The prize was managing to buy a film of the first appearance of the Soviet MiG-29 outside Russia at Kuopio Rissala in Finland, from a doctor who made documentaries. I actually met him at Bremen Airport and talked the price down using a magnificent large scarlet 1,000 Deutschmark bank note. We sold further copies to the German air force, NATO and the Israeli air attaché. (The RAF had sent a team to Finland.) However, it allowed the courses to see the new MiG, but more importantly to get an idea that the Russian pilot flew from the heart as opposed to the automaton who just obeyed orders; it was slightly scary!

When there was time off, East Friesland was a magical country and the East Frisians were the nicest and most helpful people you could ever meet. A jeweller in Jever town, Oswald Andreas, wrote a column in the local language newspaper every week comparing words in German, English, High German and English, as proof that the Frisian language was the mother tongue of English. It was hard to refute and almost certainly true. The Saxons who invaded England after the Romans left came from the European coast from modern Belgium round to Denmark. The locals were characterised by large red and oval faces of whom the Germans at large made all the racial jokes like, "Hans, look, a dead seagull". Hans looks up and says "Where?" The locals knew the best ones and when the Rhinelanders came for their holidays from the industrial Ruhr, we never stopped laughing at the straight-faced shopkeepers selling them boxes of coffee mugs with the handle on the inside and the logo 'Present from East Friesland'. The next bestseller was the backwards clock. We still have one in our kitchen.

Friesland, both Dutch and German, is totally flat. In the past the sea could come well inland so that churches were built on mounds and the farmers would drive their livestock onto these sanctuaries as the bells tolled. It could be bitterly cold so the remedy for everything seemed to be an *obstler* (fruit schnapps). The farmers lived in thatched barns, family at one end and livestock at the other. The main social activity in winter was *Bosseln,* where wooden balls were hurled down the road. It was massively skilful spinning the ball to take advantage of any camber, and you just had to get your throw beyond the other team's last ball. The locals took this very seriously and distance markers could be seen on all the minor roads. For tournaments licences were required and the fire brigade even closed off roads.

Of course, TLP had their own version of *Bosseln,* run by our Dutch sergeant major. Essentially you drank a small glass of schnapps if your team had scored, if the other team had scored or if nobody had scored for a while. Then traditionally there was a feast of fatty ham, sausages and cabbage, *Grünkohl und Pinkel* (kale and sausage), which neutralised the alcohol. It was a vicious sport. On one occasion a car arrived from German Customs and Excise to meet a Boeing 707 returning from Canada. Of course, the three customs officers could not resist the *Bosseln.* "Would you like a throw?" asked Dirk Weimer. "Oh yes please." Naturally they threw the ball far further than we could. One was coaching Roger Carr, our British navigator. He asked the boss if he was getting good advice. "Yes Roger, but fortunately you can't understand him. He hasn't realised that you are a left hander." Then the aircraft landed and they were by now a good half mile from their van. "Thank you, thanks for the schnapps." Someone called out that it was all duty-free, but they never came back.

In the winter there was also football, of course, with a thriving children's league when parents' hip flasks were actively encouraged. There was skating on frozen ponds with children's ice hockey, probably the most dangerous sport ever invented, and shopping by sledge. On a walk after a Sunday lunch on a reclaimed bit of beach, the earth and sand had been brought into 30-foot-high piles. There seemed to be a small crowd around one of them, and there was a man in a pink Edwardian flying outfit strutting round shaking hands. Sure enough, on top of the mound was a hang-glider, which he duly manned. I just had time to dive for my camera to record the crash, then sat on the ground, helpless with laughter. As the Germans started to laugh, he reappeared brushing off bits of hang-glider. One person, though, was standing not amused, my very own wife. "So how did you know he was going to crash?" "Silly sod launched crosswind." So much for the East Frisian Hang-Gliding Club.

In the summer the beaches opened up along with the rather beautiful chain of islands. Wandering, or *Wattwanderung*, over the sea bed during the short intervals when the tide was out was a regular sport. A *Friesischer Überprüfung* (like an exam) was run each weak for the tourists. "Can you milk a cow?" They had a cow simulator. "Can you vault a dyke?" A dyke was duly marked out on the ground. "Can you speak Frisian?" "Moin, Moin" would suffice, the normal daily greeting used everywhere. My James replied with some quick-fire Frisian repartee which he had learned at his German school, and the judges were so amazed that they had to invent a distinguished pass. Jever itself is a beautiful town, dominated by its castle and its association with Catherine the Great, and by the Jever brewery, producing maybe the best lager in the world.

Travel into Europe was easy. We managed to spend time in Yugoslavia as well as regular trips into the Netherlands and around north Germany. Birthday parties were considered to be incredibly important, and the barbecues ran throughout the summer, usually inviting course participants with nowhere to go. We all had commissary passes for the US Army Base Exchange at Bremerhaven to load up with monstrous steaks and Californian wine in gallon flasks. I well remember a Turkish delegation taking control of some particularly difficult American charcoal briquettes. They were horrified by the more usual Belgian method of drenching them in lighting fluid, with the small explosion that followed.

When a staff member left TLP there was invariably the *Abschiedsparty*, a sit-down dinner in a local inn, where presents, speeches and flowers featured heavily. For example, our Belgian pilot presented TLP with a print of a Belgian Mirage 5, which read,

'A perfect NATO staff officer is:
...as flexible as an American
... as humorous as a German
... as straightforward as a Brit [which worried a few Brits]
... as generous as a Dutchman
... and as sober as Belgian.

As we were hanging the picture the next morning, our new German boss, Kurt, arrived. "Ah, I did not have the chance to read this last night." He had been far too busy presenting flowers and kissing the wives. As he read his face darkened. "What's the problem?" someone asked. "I do not consider that the Germans are particularly humorous." It is just possible that this was a very subtle German joke, but I don't think so.

SCANDINAVIA

Åke Lindqvist telephoned, the Swedish Viggen pilot who I had flown on the Skyflash missile trials at Leuchars. Would I like to make an informal staff visit to Norrköping Air Force Base in southern Sweden? They would like to hear about TLP and I might like to learn more about Swedish air defence. The staff at Ramstein liked the idea, provided that it cost nothing. We would therefore make a holiday in Sweden taking the Travemünde to Malmo ferry, then driving to Stockholm via Norrköping. We would go on to stay with my cousin in western Sweden before travelling back through Denmark. What a plan. Sweden was then unknown territory. Åke proposed a two-day visit, staying on for a few days with him and his wife Karin.

Key memories stand out, starting with the briefing on how the Swedish air force operated, including fighter control radars that were retracted into the mountains. All their pilots were checked out to fly at 20 metres above the surface, flying the J37 Viggen in air defence, ground attack and reconnaissance. Norrköping had one air defence and one recce squadron. I overran my allotted time in the Viggen simulator, where holograms of Soviet types kept appearing as targets, while they insisted that there was an alternative scenario for a NATO attack. They accepted that getting used to a new type, its radar and its weapons was asking a lot, so they agreed to freeze the fuel and provide unlimited reloads of Sparrow and Sidewinder air-to-air missiles. This had to be the best arcade game ever invented until they insisted that we were late for the next event and unfroze the fuel. There was just time then to make a final intercept and recover with an autopilot approach coupled to a microwave ILS[10], landing on a motorway strip of 6,000 metres. The simulator could even cope with a reverse-thrust three-point turn to park in the forest.

The sauna was obligatory. When I queried the absence of women the answer was: "They are banned today. You can't talk flying with women around." They even opened a very old and beautiful officers' mess for a guest night, a rare event as staff were so expensive, which ended with numerous short speeches and glasses being hurled into the log fire. They would be great northern allies, and in their own words, "….and never forget the Finns". The following morning, they produced a Saab 105 for me to see the country at low level, and to find out what 20-metre flying was all about. I guess you get used to it. They liked what they heard about TLP and regretted that we could not cooperate more fully. The Saab 105? It was a friendly aircraft, very

[10] ILS is an instrument landing system whereby a bean is transmitted by ground equipment giving the pilot glide-path indications. The Swedish version was road portable.

A German air force Alpha Jet.

stable at low level with a performance not unlike a Jet Provost. The controls were not particularly responsive, but after an hour I was totally happy flying it both over the forest and in the circuit. The Viggen seemed to fly much the same as a Phantom, Åke had assured me. Tragically, I never saw him again; he passed on a couple of years later from lung cancer.

Type flying at TLP was not all front-line fighters. I clocked up a number of hours in the CT-33 (the Canadian version of the T-33 trainer). Whenever a CT-33 visited we would grab it as a radio comms jammer, playing mainly Dire Straits on the TLP radio frequencies. It was a pleasant aircraft to fly with responsive controls, with excellent lookout, but maybe just a little underpowered. The German Alpha Jets were regular attenders on TLP courses, but they were unimpressive. They were delightful small dancing machines, well flown by the Germans, but with an unimpressive air-to-ground weapons suite. The BAE Hawk, conversely, made several visits as enemy air from the tactical weapons unit at RAF Chivenor, whose wartime role would be supporting air defence, armed with two Sidewinders and a 30-mm cannon. In fact, I once flew in an Alpha Jet and a Hawk on adjacent days. Frankly the Alpha belonged in a flying club or maybe a training school as used by the French and Belgians. The Hawk was a rugged little war machine with a great turning performance and, for its size, well-armed. What it lacked was a radar-warning receiver as it was all too easy to engage when on a visual combat air patrol.

A RAF Hawk T.1 of No. 1 TWU.

The Jaguar and Harrier made regular appearances, but both were limited, the Harrier by range and weapons load and the Jaguar was noticeably underpowered although pleasant enough to fly. When fully loaded, for example with a reconnaissance pod on a hot day, it needed the curve of the earth to achieve flight and a hard turn was difficult. The Belgian Mirage 5s were, frankly, considered to be more effective war machines, but with more primitive weapon aiming. The Lightning was, frankly,

A Belgian air force Mirage 5.

A USAF F-15A.

outclassed. While the Phantoms and Starfighters made steady appearances. The Wittmund Wing, our Frisian neighbours, (JG 71 Richthofen) even produced a scarlet and white F-4F Phantom to commemorate the 35 years since their re-establishment.

At the other end of the scale, the USAF F-15 and the multi-nation F-16s made regular appearances. The F-15 is a heavyweight, immensely armed and capable all-

Author pictured with Captain Jim Downey (USAF) after flying in the back seat of a F-15B following a successful sortie.

weather fighter. It even has grab handles welded into the cockpit to enable the pilot to pull himself around to see over his shoulder. The track-while-scan (TWS) radar enhancement was fitted over a weekend when we had a two-seat F-15B at Jever, and it worked first time. I managed to get the TWS pictures before the aircraft was declared NOFORN at the lunchtime after I had flown in the aircraft. In many ways it is a next-generation Phantom, or as my office USAF partner said: "You surely can tell who its daddy is!"

The F-16 was and is a different story. Its phased array radar has been 'state of the art' for 40 years, and I flew back seat in the F-16A on a number of occasions. It was a dream. The 30-degree reclining seat allows G to be pulled in comparative comfort up to a survivable 9 G, and since the US Air National Guard received its F-16As and Bs, the addition of the AIM-7 Sparrow missile had made it a top air superiority fighter for American homeland air defence. The CF-18B, however, which I flew at Bad Solingen in exchange for an intelligence briefing, was just a little heavy on the controls. You could tell that a computer was helping to deliver an acceptable 'feel'. So, do I have a favourite? Well of course, it used to be the Hawker Hunter, but since my first F-16B flight there has been no contest, even the heavier USAF F-16D. What a jet.

A year after my trip to Sweden we agreed to house-sit for a friend who had a NATO appointment in Denmark. This coincided with a Danish F-35 Draken team from Karup AFB in Jutland making a guest appearance at TLP. One of the pilots was Jan,

A RCAF CF-18A flying over Bad Solingen.

A Danish F-35 flying over Aalborg, Denmark.

who I had met in Sardinia, as an exchange pilot flying the Jaguar. He invited me to Karup to fly the two-seater F-35. I was amazed that the mission would be a gun-armed recce flight over the Baltic. Their boss's last words were: "If you end up in the sea and are rescued by the East Germans, just keep saying 'Sköl', and we'll send someone from the embassy." He was serious. Now, of course, the Saab Draken was a highly effective lightweight fighter, according to the Swedes and the Finns. However, the aileron springs in the Danish recce F-35 had been stiffened for the recce role to make a more stable photographic platform, so it was just that. We took pictures of some Russian corvettes, identified by their red decks, and we overflew the Danish island of Bornholm to assure them that democracy was in safe hands. I loved it all. It was a great and unexpected day.

TACTICAL AIR MEET 1986 (TAM86), KLEINE-BROGEL, BELGIUM

The tactical air meet for the NATO AAFCE took place in the June of 1986 at a Belgian air force base, situated at Kleine-Brogel in Flanders. Teams flew in from most of the air wings in the Second and Fourth Allied Tactical Air Forces. Around 60 aircraft would fly daily on simulated strikes into France, with the air-defence fighters escorting and sweeping ahead for the TAM86 attack aircraft. They would be supported by a NATO E-3A Sentry (AWACS)[11] flying from Geilenkirchen and actually registered as a Luxembourg military aircraft. The daily opposition would be 40 fighters of the French air force including the Mirage 2000 with a look-down shoot-down Pulse Doppler capability.

The AAFCE headquarters staff would set the daily tasks and handle the debriefs and lessons learnt afterwards. Rob (our Canadian CF-104 pilot) and I were invited along as observers. This really was TLP on a grand scale, and I guess we saw ourselves as the specialists, ready to offer unrequested advice. The visiting air and ground crews were accommodated in half of the nearby Center Parcs. In the adjacent bungalows were the French Mirage F1 air-defence team, of whom only the colonel spoke some English. With a French linguist qualification, I quickly became their interpreter. It was an opportunity to speak aeronautical French again.

In fact, Rob and I had a private agenda. For some time TLP air defence had been working on a possible Central Region scenario with tactics that might integrate all the emerging radar systems that could see the low-level air battle as well as the fighters that would rely on them, many of whom had a look-down-shoot-down capability. We already knew that it worked, but only with comparatively small numbers of fighters and attack aircraft. This was a chance to prove it on a much larger scale and offer it as a link between any fighter sweep and the lead attack elements. Essentially, we had a system whereby the attackers would know where the enemy air-defence fighters were waiting. And, of course, working with the home team would be the NATO E-3A Sentry (AWACS), whose operators by now knew exactly what we were doing. It was a little disappointing that the AAFCE staff attitude was "OK, by all means see if the attackers want to use it". Air defence was already convinced, as were the AWACS crews. There was a slow take-up as we tried to flog our wares. "Well, OK, we'll give it a try", to a couple of strangers in flying suits.

A bit later on one of the ex-Second World War Luftwaffe pilots told us that he had heard about our magic air-defence grid. It was certainly an old colleague of Oberst Klaffenbach, probably General Hohagen. The grid of course had involved too many people and was open knowledge. The tactics used were classified. "You realise, I suppose, that you have re-invented the air-defence strategy used by the Luftwaffe in 1943 to defeat the streams of bombers using chaff and electronic jamming?" These were the Tame Boar (using fighter control) and Wild Boar (free fighter inside the

[11] The NATO E-3A Sentry (AWACS) is a long set of initials for a Boeing 707 or C-135 modified with a large disc housing a Pulse Doppler radar.

box) tactics, similar but by no means identical. It was interesting though that we had come close to their historic system.

Well, it worked. The French opposition were swept away, and the 'mud-movers' (ground-attack crews) were sold on the geographical grid, the air-defence concept handed to us by the AAFCE four-star general. The AWACS had reported far ahead and the sweep escort fighters had reported back accurately. We would do it again the next day. Unknown to us, though, the AAFCE staff produced a second AWACS to support the French air defence, and it all worked again. The AAFCE staff debriefs though were disappointing, usually starting off with a joke that could not be translated into French, and drawing few lessons or conclusions. Rob and I had complained. Be careful what you wish for. On day three, just after take-off, there was a mid-air collision between a Belgian Mirage 5 and a French Jaguar. The French pilot died.

We knew none of this. The 92 Squadron detachment commander had offered me his slot in the fighter escort and I was already airborne. We had flown into a French Mirage 2000 patrol at 90 degrees, and had claimed kills on them all. As Red 2, I had time to make a sighting solution on all four Mirages; totally unrealistic of course, as for real, after the first missile, the Mirage formation would have broken up. When we landed, we heard about the collision, and a few minutes later Rob and I were tasked by the AAFCE staff with producing the debrief. "OK, but we need four hours to prepare." "Too bad, you have two." When I stood up in front of 200 aircrew in a frosty silence and explained the first engagement with Red 2's quite unrealistic claims of four Mirages engaged, the French visiting colonel stood up and, looking around, asked, "Who was Red 2?" "Colonel, sorry to disappoint, but it was me." Afterwards I could have run for French president as they spoke about the respect shown to their dead colleague. Phew! The next day, though, at the briefing, when it got to the point of deciding which AAFCE general would fly in the home team French F1D, their colonel stood up and announced, "No, today I fly Al". Not a great career move, as it turned out.

The Dassault Mirage F1 was simply the most beautiful aircraft to fly. It had a massive engine, pulse radar (which meant no look-down shoot-down), four air-to-air missiles, of which two were radar seeking and two were infrared, and a cannon. The colonel explained: "It is a massive aircraft but with a tiny weapons system." It positively danced with fingertip control, tight turning, but essentially, at low level, a day fighter just a bit like a modern-day Spitfire. We ended up close to Luxembourg, then climbed out and flew back to Belgium. The generals were unforgiving, but it was worth it for the chance to fly this lovely iconic aircraft.

BERLIN, TUCSON AND BELENKO

TLP ground school took up a lot of our time, covering multiple topics and keeping them all up to date. I had expanded my bit of ground school to encompass Soviet weapons and tactics and inevitably that led to the quality training and skill of the Soviet pilot. I had been reading every book I could find on Russian history, religion, politics and way of life, and had come to a book by a Soviet defector to the West, Viktor Suvorov, called *Inside the Soviet Army.* He explained that the West had it all wrong, that we saw the Central Region threat as a massive Soviet air army supported in some way by the East European air forces. Now recount the East Europeans in the same Order of Battle as the Soviets and you'll see a complete second air army. In Berlin, at the 6912 ESG (Electronic Support Group – a large radar perched on top of the Teufelsberg; the massive mound of rubble from Berlin's wartime destruction) where I went quarterly to join the American team evaluating the last quarter's air activities in East Germany, one of the Americans visiting from one of the US intelligence agencies knew Suvorov. He agreed that his first book was highly accurate then, but after that he started writing for the money. Back in Jever via the American military train to Bremerhaven, we did recount the opposition and he was absolutely correct.

So, one line of research led to another. I briefed NATO crews on the Soviet massive set-piece exercises where everything was choreographed and on the way that crews briefed and trained for missions, no deviation permitted. I had even managed to borrow a full Soviet flying kit which one of the RAF clerks would model for us. Viktor Belenko – another Soviet defector – had described this in detail in his book, *MiG Pilot*, before he flew his MiG-25 to Japan. I had heard stories though, of sightings of Soviet aircraft flying under bridges on the way back from their bombing ranges, and I began to suspect that there was much more to the Soviet pilot than we had been told. In fact, the Soviet lecture became a major export which I was able to trade, for example with the Canadians at Bad Solingen in exchange for the CF-18B ride. They even sent a CT-33 as a taxi.

Shortly after that we hosted a US Air National Guard (ANG) group at TLP and on 15 November 1984 I was in the back of an LTV A-7K Corsair in a flight of two, intent on DACT with a pair of Dutch F-16s. The A-7 was wonderfully light on the controls and the air guards were certain that they could beat an F-16 from a slow-speed start. We pulled up in line abreast with each F-16 on the outsides, 60 degrees up and commenced at about 150 kts. It probably took the Dutch three-quarters of a high-G barrel-roll attack, each to be in a gun-firing position behind the A-7s. We

A Portuguese TA-7P.

did this twice before the Americans were convinced but, in the meantime, I had just met in the A-7 a lovely surprisingly delicate fighter that flew beautifully despite its ugliness. (It was nicknamed the SLUF – Short, Little, Ugly, F*****.) I did have another chance later on in 1986 to fly the Portuguese TA-7P, a very serious TLP attack mission, but the same delightful aircraft.

This was also my introduction to the ANG, who came over to Jever several times with their A-7s. Each US State fielded two ANG squadrons, and while a part of the USAF order of battle, they were spread through the various air force roles and answerable to the state governor. They were much more relaxed and free thinking than the USAF we were used to, which worried the American with whom I shared an office. However, they were deeply interested in all things Soviet, which led to an invitation to bring the Soviet briefing out to Arizona, all (unavoidable) expenses paid, to a two-week symposium at Tucson and Davis-Monthan AFBs, run by the 152nd Fighter Squadron who were also the ANG Transition Training School for the A-7. My TLP German lieutenant colonel decided that it was essential that he came too but never could explain why.

At the beginning of September 1984, we drove from Jever to RAF Laarbruch. The RAF had agreed to take the good lieutenant colonel on board a VC10 to RAF Brize Norton, as the Germans would bring us back. We then took a hire car to RAF Scampton where we joined the crew of a Kansas ANG KC-135 tanker flying home the next day to Topeka, Kansas. The trip's highlight was flying the refuelling boom which was remarkably sensitive. I had been on the receiving end of a KC-135 previously, where a 13-ft metal adaptor hose was fixed onto the boom for our probe refuelling. Not only was disengaging tricky to take out the kink in the hose, but the boom operator also made engagement problematic by trying to help, flying the hose onto the probe. "That's right," said our boomer, "the navy are always complaining about that."

The highlight of a Sunday stopover in the Mid-West, where everything was closed, was a jazz bar on the outskirts of Topeka. As we entered. the music stopped and the atmosphere froze. It was time to be very European. They eventually accepted that we

The author (left) with members of the Air National Guard in Tucson, Arizona.

liked jazz and wanted a beer. Jazz and good fellowship mattered. These were great people who loved a night out, and even looked after our air force car for us. The Americans said the next day that we were lucky to get out alive, but we had spent one of the best nights ever there. In the morning an ANG C-130 called in on its way to Tucson and we slept all the way.

For the first week I flew every day, three times in the A-7K and twice in the F-16B on bombing and gunnery flights. The A-7s had moved to nearby Davis-Monthan AFB for the symposium. One A-7K flight was devoted to anti-SAM tactics, flying at ultra-low level over the Sonoran Desert, 480 knots at 200 feet as I remember. I would call out a SAM launch and the pilot reacted viciously moving the A-7 first vertically then rolling into a second plane at 90 degrees. In the days before thrust vectoring that was enough to fool a SAM. Another flight was DACT with an ANG F-15A Eagle. Actually, we were holding our own when the A-7 flicked into a spin. My guard pilot was totally unimpressed so we split again for another engagement. The result was the same and we spun once more. "Do you think that the vast ECM pod on one of the wing pylons was the problem?" I asked. "Not a chance. You have a go." So, we spun for the third time and with a standard recovery the A-7 came straight out of the spin, check yaw, full opposite rudder, stick centrally forward and prepare to eject. As we walked in, he asked "What was that you were saying about the ECM pod?"

All I remember of the third A-7 flight was the recovery into Davis-Monthan. Flying with a pilot who I flew with at TLP called 'Wizard', I was on the recovery to pitch into the circuit and land. Now, with its warm dry climate, Davis-Monthan

An ANG A-7 at Davis-Monthan AFB.

is also the home of the US Forces 'boneyard'. There were something like 6,000 military aircraft laid out in rows on a vast area of desert. For example, there were new rows of AV-8As and more B-52s and F-4s than you could count. (The RAF F-4Js were recovered from here, reconditioned and put back to work.) As I rolled out down wind, Wizard said "Do you see what I see?" There was a large maintenance hangar at the centre of the 'boneyard', and on its concrete apron stood a neat line of seven or eight black F-19s, the aircraft that did not apparently exist, despite the rumours. Airfix had produced a 1:72 kit. There was even a 19 model in the amazing Pima Air Museum. When we walked into ops, we each drew what we'd seen, and we had surely looked at the same aircraft. When we drove over there a little later the F-19s had gone. Your explanation is as good as any. The F-19 was clearly a very comprehensive programme of disinformation to cover the development of the F-117, but maybe the F-19 had existed after all; or maybe they were just bits of fibreglass to fool the satellites.

At the weekend there was some heated discussion amongst the guards. Viktor Belenko was coming for the weekend and would address the symposium the following week. Someone had to take care of him for the weekend. He was the Soviet defector mentioned earlier who had given the USA the rare gift of an operational MiG-25 Foxbat supersonic air-defence fighter. He apparently had characteristic Russian tolerance to alcohol and nobody wanted to be involved. There was no problem, apparently, with a Brit being officer in charge of Viktor, so we set off into Tucson in a large blue USAF car and an address and time for the Sunday evening barbecue. "What sort of music do you like Viktor?" "Country and Western." And so the evening started.

It was a magical tour around every Country and Western bar in Tucson. In the process, Viktor told me everything I wanted to know about Soviet military flying. We discussed the working day from breakfast onwards, and it was quite true that their flying was heavily scripted. We talked about the influence of the regimental commissar and the KGB. They would take a young pioneer (a sort of boy scout) and massage his entire career including flying training and squadron service. You never knew for sure who you were sharing a room with. Viktor had been an Aero L-29 (Delphín) flying instructor and we even got down to teaching techniques on the more difficult exercises. It became clear that the Soviet was taught, as I had suspected, to fly from the heart, which was born out over the following years as we got to know them better. The MiG-25 was a monster, but a very potent and capable long-range point-defence fighter.

At some point Viktor asked where the staff car was. We had abandoned it somewhere in Tucson, and carried on in taxis. He also had no idea where he was staying, but there was an empty room next to mine in the bachelor officer quarters. On the Sunday, we eventually found the car and even arrived on time at the barbecue. He was once again Victor Smith from Great Falls, Montana, although he may have changed identity on the way home. Despite all this, he was unable to discuss the Rodina without a tear, the umbilical that all Russians feel with the Motherland.

The symposium briefing was a great success and the guard even paid for airline tickets back to Washington DC, where we picked up the regular GAF Boeing 707 trooper back to Cologne. The day after, I was at RAF Wildenrath once again, flying the Phantom in a Third World War exercise, back in the Cold War. My single souvenir is a copy of *MiG Pilot*, bought for me by a sympathetic Air Guard wife, signed: "To my friend Al, with best wishes from Victor Belenko." A year or so later, the brand-new MiG-29 Fulcrum was displayed as a five-aircraft aerobatic team in Finland at Kuopio Rissala as already described on page 49. We were later able to obtain a film of the display with the Russian radio soundtrack, and it was clear that these were no automatons. Official intelligence was sometimes very wrong.

Back to work and I was at the RAFG headquarters at RAF Rheindahlen, about 10 km from Wildenrath. It was a Friday afternoon, NAAFI shopping complete and I was receiving my intelligence briefing before heading back to Jever. I asked the group captain giving the brief about the new post they were trying to establish in Berlin; a sort of small-scale intelligence evaluation unit based on the RAF radar squadron at RAF Gatow. "We've got it established." "What's the job spec?" I asked

The author at RAAF Butterworth with a Mirage IIID.

The author at Butterworth for the South East Asia Air Defence course.

just out of interest. "An air defence squadron leader, conversant ground attack and knowledgeable recce and intel analysis," he told me. "Of course, he doesn't exist but we'll take the closest we can get." "What do you mean, he doesn't exist?" "It's you, isn't it? Do you want the job?" "You could say that. Yes please."

On the following Monday, they called for a few details and told me that they had written to personnel. I phoned home with the news that we were off to Berlin to a dream job. Then half an hour later, our AAFCE air marshal called. "Great news, I've got you a job at Cranwell in the Department of Air Warfare." He was trying to help sadly, but that was it. Department of Air Warfare – I loathed the place. I had no respect for the incoming boss, and it was mutual. I was lecturing on subjects where up-to-date lecture content was impossible and there was always somebody who was a specialist in the subject. I learned the full horrors of manufactured intelligence to achieve policy issues, while spending every spare moment on DIY in our house that had been let out for ten years.

However, I had a reserve commitment to fly the Phantom at Wildenrath for a week every six months. To keep current I flew the air cadets on the Chipmunk at RAF Newton, and scrounged as many weather checks as I could in the Jet Provost T.5A at Cranwell's flying training school. Every six months I went to Butterworth in Malaysia to lecture the (five-power) South East Asian Air Defence organisation, which I loved. I even traded a lecture with the Australians for a flight in their Mirage IIID (D for deux places; their squadron aircraft was the IIIO, I guess O for Oz.) What an interesting aircraft. It flew a little like the Phantom, heavy-ish, but with an effective radar, gun and missiles, but no look-shoot shoot-down capability. It had a good turning performance, excellent power-to-weight ratio, and it was a fighter that instilled confidence, as did the entire Mirage range. I landed from the back seat in rain without problem.

A nice interlude was an invitation to go to RAF Shawbury and lecture aspiring candidates for the promotion exams on air defence. I was able to trade this for a Gazelle taxi ride there and back, always enjoyable when you don't have to learn the checks or worry about red lights. I had set the air defence question on passive defence (hardened shelters, gas masks etc.) in the last ten minutes of a long lecture when they had stopped listening. I also managed a flight in the Tornado F.2 at RAF Coningsby, which was a little disappointing. It was the interim aircraft prior to the F.3, but there were vast spaces in the aircraft for equipment that wasn't yet ready, and the radar was

The author with Fred Grundy after flying a Tornado F.2.

a joke. We had previously had a pair flying as enemy air at Jever; almost non-effective. I found four aircraft in one of the Wash bombing ranges, and managed to insert them into the radar computer. Then as they turned onto their bombing runs, each contact went contrast inverted until they reappeared as the aircraft came head on. When the screen was full of contrast inverted contacts, Fred, my instructor, explained that this was just one of the problems. "Now clear the lot and start again." Additionally, there was no height finding, and it is frankly amazing that there were no mid-air collisions in the F.2's early days. The performance was unimpressive but of course this was in reality a modified Tornado GR.1, purpose-built for the attack role. The F.3 was essentially an uprated F.2. At the end of the F.3's life, everything worked, but it took a long time to get there.

Every time I drove home, I watched the GR.1s flying around RAF Cottesmore, just off the A1. After a major fall-out with the DAW boss, I requested an instructor posting there, switching to specialist aircrew, and with a sigh of relief arrived at the Tornado Tri-National Training Establishment (TTTE), to start the type conversion and join the staff.

CHAPTER TEN

THE TORNADO

RAF COTTESMORE, 1988

The Tornado GR.1 was a remarkably successful aircraft in RAF service and – aged 50 at the time of writing – still serves the German air force. It was produced and built by the British, Germans and Italians, to deliver twice the bomb load of an Avro Lancaster with devastating accuracy. The work share was British and Germans 40 per cent each and the Italians 20 per cent. The Germans quite rightly demanded that the radar should be theirs, despite having virtually no avionics industry, then promptly sub-contracted to Texas Instruments. The radar was the heart of the aircraft and performed brilliantly. The navigation and weapon-aiming computer had a memory of just 64 KB, about the same time as the Commodore 64 became available. The supporting navigation-planning computer, which wheezed and clanked, was the size of a phone box and the discs were ten-inch floppies. At the time all these were futuristic. Any planned routes were downloaded to a tape cassette that was inserted into the aircraft, which happily could also play music. In fact, one of the findings after a crew ejection from a Tornado F.3 in Cyprus was that the crew were listening to a Dire Straits cassette.

The Tornado's design was intriguing. The underneath of the fuselage was wide and flat in order to carry the various runway denial weapons such as the JP233 and MW-1. The wing pylons supported either fuel tanks of bombs with AIM-9 Sidewinder air-to-air missiles filled to the side of the pylons. A large bomb load could be carried on the multiple pylons. Computer-enhanced controls and negative stability were still in the future, so the configuration could be changed by variable-sweep wings. The GR.1 wings were cleared for three positions, 25 degrees for circuit work, 45 degrees for operational usage and 67 degrees for high speed. You got used to sweeping the wings remarkably quickly. The actual flying controls were quite complex with an automatic interface between flaps and wing sweep, as well as airbrakes mounted above the fuselage The engines were a little disappointing with a complex three-spool configuration and a maximum of 13,500 rpm. These were not the massive General Electric engines fitted to American and Soviet fighters with high bypass ratios and ability to withstand damage, but they worked and were economical. The Texas Instruments radar had a highly effective terrain-following capability. Of course, the offensive air policy at the time was for low-level ingress which remained to the start of the first Gulf War. It was a nice aeroplane to fly from either cockpit.

The TTTE had opened for business in 1981 at RAF Cottesmore in Rutland, UK. Cottesmore had been on care and maintenance for a number of years so making it Tornado-ready was reasonably straight-forward. It needed a new apron to the east of the hangars and squadron accommodation was needed in front of two of the large hangars. All maintenance would be by the RAF, so a small house was built in front of the hangars for a small number of German and Italian logisticians to convert RAF maintenance records to the parent paperwork. There were separate safety equipment sections. The national mix would be 40 per cent German and British and 20 per

A Tornado GR.1 returning to base over the Alps.

cent Italian, with a slight bias for the Germans, who would train for the air force and navy. Personnel would live in married quarters if they so choose, (the Italians did, the Germans less so) and the NAAFI was split to enable duty-free sales. The working language would be English, but there would be a German and Italian colonel to ensure fair balance. The post of chief flying instructor would rotate. It worked well.

TTTE needed three small flying squadrons to make it work, one each run by the participating air forces. Ideally, they were the same, but inevitably each took on its national characteristics. There was also a ground school squadron that managed all the classroom and the simulator training. The fourth flying squadron was called Standards, looking after the professional development of the instructional staff. I turned up late on day one having received no joining instructions, and failing to guess that the reporting time was 08.10. The station commander knew me of old and was somewhat annoyed. No problem; I was just so happy to be away from Cranwell, and a 30-minute drive from home. However, the ground school was difficult. The aircraft systems were comparatively futuristic, and it took a long time to become familiar with the cockpit checks and then the aircraft emergencies. I was crewed with Franz, a young German navigator, but we cooperated well and after two weeks passed all the exams and simulator checks, and then reported to the bar to meet our instructors. We were going to C (Italian) Squadron, and my instructor would be their boss. I had no idea that he was himself under review, and after two trips I had a new instructor, and the boss was on his way back to Italy. I thought he was great to fly with, but what did I know? So, my first Tornado GR.1 flight was with an Italian instructor in a German aircraft. There were small aircraft differences which did help later on, but that was in the future.

After ground school came the aircraft conversion, five flights with an instructor pilot (IP) then a check flight, followed by a flight with a staff navigator. After that came the great day when you flew with your student navigator, at the same time passing an instrument rating check, getting familiar with the navigation systems and mastering close and battle formation. Then the navigation got more difficult, with planning bombing attacks at low level, the terrain-following radar was introduced and then the whole package was put together at night. After three months a pairs attack by two aircraft on three targets were all planned from scratch. The entire event took four hours and the course ended with the student crew running the entire flight. At this stage, the Brits went off to RAF Honington for live weapons and tactics training, the Germans went to Jever and the Italians to Ghedi, near Lake Como. I was staying on, so I could relax now, could I not?

I was not allowed to relax. On the Monday morning, I was back in ground school on a one-week course designed to train Tornado instructor pilots and navigators. Very few IPs were 'proper' qualified flying instructors with the full rigours of the Central Flying School behind us and, in fact, there were half a dozen of us as well as a German who had done a basic instructing tour in the States. We noticed after a while that when a student was having trouble, he was passed to one of us. However, the treaty did not allow for QFIs and we were all treated as IPs and competent to instruct. After the one week of ground school, we simply had to convert to the back seat and fly a very reduced syllabus with the Standards squadron before being let loose on an actual student.

RUTLAND'S AIR FORCE

I was now an instructor on A Squadron, the boss was a German navy lieutenant commander, and the flavour was distinctly German. The crew room was built like a miniature beer hall which invariably opened on the last landing. Birthdays were never forgotten. The boss showed me how to loop a Tornado at 67 degrees wing sweep using F-104 speeds. I seem to remember that the loop went from 5,000 ft topping out at 18,000 ft, which appealed to the German sense of humour. In the summer we had a squadron treasure hunt, once on bicycles. Then in the winter we participated in *Bosseln* around the perimeter road just as we had at Jever. Apart from that, the syllabus really only took three months to complete and afterwards the courses just kept recycling. At one stage RAF management decided that I should drop some bombs, and arranged for me to fly from Honington for a couple of days. The gods of war were unimpressed though, and for two days running all the UK's bombing ranges filled up with cloud, I never flew a bombing mission and I was allowed to go home.

The TTTE students were nationally very different. The British youngsters had survived training and arrived competent as expected. A few were totally excellent. The Italians had in some cases trained in the States but they had all flown in European conditions on return and were invariably surprisingly good. I flew with one on his conversion but never bothered again; no challenge. Even the young Italian navigators, who had flown a mere 100 hours in a USAF Boeing T-43 navigation trainer, were superb. The German students were generally a little underconfident. On the post-ground school beer call, there they were in their beautiful grey leather jackets, covered in meretricious badges. I would count the badges and opt for the boy with the most, as he would be quite the hardest to train. A number of older pilots came through from all three nations converting to the Tornado, but they were always fun.

Just occasionally we received a student from another service embarking on an exchange tour. I drew the French Étendard pilot from the French navy, going to one of the German marine air wings in Schleswig-Holstein. We had received no training records, and our Italian CFI wanted an instructor with French in reserve. *Lui-même* was brilliant and fantastically rewarding to fly with. Then at the post-conversion beer call, our station commander came into our chat with really awful French. "Oh, sorry Al, we're talking French." "*Pas de problème*." My French protégé reacted accordingly: "Oh, sorry Sir, we're speaking French." Another great career move. Actually, not really.

So, we usually flew front seat with a student navigator and gradually became confident enough to debrief their attack films. Before that Bryan Murphy, a staff navigator who I had first met at Kleine-Brogel singing his heart out, would quietly assist. Then when it was time to teach the course terrain-following radar techniques (in other words low-level radar plugged in, 500 feet above ground level at 420 knots) there were never quite enough staff navigators. There were only about 12 in total. Quite incredibly on a dark night one of our Tornados had collided with a Marham aircraft, and the crew were dead; statistically quite impossible, but it had happened. We were then immediately restricted to a long formation with aircraft four minutes apart, known as an 'Iron Gorilla' (see also p.148). Timing was tight as we traversed the low-flying areas (LFA). We had to be clear of one LFA before any Honington aircraft or any other night predator was allowed in. So, the call went out for pilots to fly in the back. That was OK, except that if you wanted a control column then you had one less television display and a set of fairly primitive instruments in lieu. Normally the back seat had two television displays for three main requirements: navigation, fixing position and attack. With a single stick there was just the one display, so it was the devil's choice. I chose to have the stick. Bryan was always there to jump on any sign of weakness and I enjoyed it all.

Flying with another staff pilot was always good value. I spent an hour with an Italian staff pilot teaching him how to fly air-defence intercepts. This was tricky since, while the radar could be put into a B-scan mode (all angles off the nose now in parallel lines) a lock was not a feature. However, we stationed ourselves near the Wash and made several good intercepts of passing aircraft. On another occasion we had to collect an aircraft that was stranded at what's left of RAF Biggin Hill after an air show. London Radar gave us a direct clearance over London at 2,000 feet, but the weather was foul. No matter, I was in the back and managed to bring up a perfect picture of the Thames which could have been straight from *Eastenders*.

Flying with a staff navigator was a revelation. They were highly knowledgeable and skilled in all levels of air-to-ground flying. You could relax and they would think of everything, including map reading. That was until the day of the Leuchars funeral. There was no pressure on the aircraft at the time, and my Italian chief instructor gave me permission to take a Tornado to Leuchars for the day. "Who would like to come?" One of the German navigators said he would love to and off we went. On arrival in the cross-servicing flight, I had to hurry. I last saw him in the ground crew tea bar, feet up on their table, reading *Sporting Life* in front of the afternoon's horse racing. "Leave it all to me."

Well, he was still there when I got back a few hours later. The ground crew apologised. They had done all they could, but there were a few outstanding items. "He's been sitting there all afternoon Sir." We had to get the aircraft back to Cottesmore for night flying so we set off on a low-level cross-country through the Pentland Hills. He was calling the turns quite effectively until we turned into a steep valley and I was confronted with a vertical cliff face. So, afterburners in, and a pull-up into the vertical. Unfortunately, we were beneath the Glasgow air traffic zone so it was time to invert the aircraft, pull over the top of the mountain and level the wings going down the other side. Of course, as we went over the top there was a car park and everyone seemed to have their camera out. We waited a week to see if there was any fuss, but in the meantime, he was quite proud to be the 'laziest navigator in the world'.

The social scene was incredible. There were three formal events amongst the flying staff. The Brits produced a Burns Night in January, loved and misunderstood by all. In the summer the Italians produced an Italian Night, each of which focused on a different area of Italy with decorations, food and music; utterly wonderful and magical occasions. We still have three china plates hanging in our kitchen with Italian recipes. The Italians really were absolute perfectionists. The Germans, however, foreswore subtlety and recreated a Munich Oktoberfest in the vacated motor transport hangar, where beer was served from watering cans and schnapps from large kitchen jugs into miniature tankards hung round the neck. An oompah band was flown in a few days in advance, actually a Luftwaffe military band, but they were total pros and could play anything. In fact, the locals loved them as they set up band concerts over the weekend in Stamford and Oakham. The entire station attended the Oktoberfest, then spent the next 11 months waiting for the next one.

Then there were the 'Landaways'. We actually did have a wartime role and that was to deliver aircraft as they were needed, using civil airways. The Germans and Italians were not remotely interested, so we hard-pressed Brits took their weekends away in Spain and Portugal as well as Italy and Germany. In fact, these were not just cultural multipliers but also incredible learning events for looking after the aircraft. The Tornado had actually been designed with a container to collect all gun bullet cases for recycling. The space was exactly right for two aircrew holdalls with some extra space where the guns would have been. We managed to get to the Italian lakes a few times, and to the open-air opera in Verona, sitting on Roman stone benches alongside the chorus of Hebrew Slaves in an unforgettable performance of Verdi's *Aida*.

Conversely Tito, my Portuguese friend from Jever gave us an unforgettable weekend in Lisbon. It worked out well as long as we had the aircraft back in time for the second wave at Cottesmore thinking about where we might go next time. Portugal was initially a real challenge as nobody knew anything about the place. We took two aircraft into RAF St Mawgan to refuel before setting out. While we were there a flight of navy Hunters arrived and I sat in one thinking "What a wreck. Was I seriously in love with it?" Once airborne in the Tornados, we headed for Monte Real, home of Portugal's A-7Ps and found nothing but help and professionalism.

Shortly after, a German student, flying on one of the other squadrons with a brand-new Italian staff navigator, flew right across Leicester Airport at 500 feet. I took the phone call quite by chance. In fact, the Leicester Aero Club was pretty reasonable. "Just tell us next time that you're coming." I invited them to visit Cottesmore, which they did. They invited us to take part in their club navigation competition the following weekend. We then did take part with Kevin, a fellow Cottesmore QFI, as navigator, when neither of us had the first idea what was involved. I checked out on the Cessna 172 with the idea that we would fly our sons in the back. We missed the first clue totally, not believing that anything could be so slow, then got the rest. We were just a few seconds out in overhead arrival time, thanks to Kevin, with the next pilot several minutes late. We came second, which we discovered at the ball that evening in the Grand Hotel, Leicester. Then my lovely wife drew her own ticket for the star prize in the raffle and the chairman asked us not to come back. "Unless," he said, "you've got a spare instructor rating and come and work for us." Well, that led to several more wonderful years of civil aero club instructing, as well as a great relationship between the Leicester Aero Club and Cottesmore.

Guy, one of our A Squadron instructors, was 50 years old and harboured a secret ambition to train as a fully qualified instructor. He had been the unit maintenance test pilot at RAF St Athan, and it was he who claimed to have landed a Beaver at 90 degrees across the 300-metre runway width during a storm at RAF St Mawgan. We believed him. CFS accepted him and off he went. Three months later Guy called to say that he had successfully finished the course with a couple of hours to spare, so would I like to come to Scampton and fly the Tucano with him. Of course.

The Tucano, a Brazilian turbo-prop with advertised jet-handling qualities, was the successor to the venerable Jet Provost. It was a lovely light and easy aircraft to fly, with nice tight aerobatics, but the elephant in the cockpit was what was known as the 'Banana Switch', a horizontal rocker on the front of the throttle for manually applying yaw trim as airflow was altered over the rudder either by speed or engine power. It was a joke. The Swiss Pilatus PC-9 was a similar aircraft, where yaw was applied automatically. This was simply not a jet-handling quality. The Tucano was really a political buy to keep Shorts alive in Belfast. Even then, half the aircraft assembled there were hangar queens until a young engineering officer spotted that the unserviceable aircraft were all registered with even numbers. The story turned out to be true, as one production line at Shorts was manned by Shorts's highly skilled workforce while the other line was rather less qualified. That said, when the problems were sorted out the Tucano was a popular machine giving years of good service. I also managed a flight at RAF Leeming in the back of an air-defence Tornado F.3, another highly political aircraft. Unsurprisingly, it flew just like its close relative, the Tornado GR.1 attack aircraft, but of course had more powerful engines and could fly a lot faster.

The TTTE stood down in 1999. Its aircraft were 20 years old, and ready for a midlife update. However, all three national updates would be different, catering for new weapons, hardware and software. A combined training would no longer be feasible, and so this unique organisation would close. The aircraft re-emerged as the Tornado GR.4 and all conversion training eventually moved to RAF Lossiemouth. The Harriers returning from Germany moved into Cottesmore.

THE RUSSIANS

Shortly after my 50th birthday a young German pilot on one of the other squadrons tried to kill us both. I had agreed to do an instrument rating for them, at night in fact, which included flying a toss-bombing release at 60 degrees nose high. This was to simulate a high pull-up in order to throw the weapon forwards while the Tornado made its escape. It was a tricky evening with a mixture of stars and fishing boats in the Wash and he totally lost control. We ended up pointing vertically downwards into the Wash, when I took control and recovered the aircraft. By the time we had practised the manoeuvre a few times then flown home, I had decided to leave the RAF, to fly a light twin-engine aircraft commercially, like a Cessna 426. In addition to TTTE, I was flying at Leicester at weekends and with No. 7 Air Experience Flight at RAF Newton flying cadets from the Air Training Corps in the wonderful and venerable Chipmunk. A very different flying future for a middle-aged head case was beckoning. However, before that came the Russians.

The Russian air force aerobatic team, the Russian Knights, had brought their Sukhoi Su-27 team to RAF Scampton, hosted by the Red Arrows. They had been generous flying RAF aircrew in their two-seater, and it had been decided that they would have two flights in the back of a Tornado. The two senior RAF pilots at Cottesmore would fly them, and I got a call the evening before to ask if I would like to take a spare aircraft and a day out with the Russians. I went with Bryan and indeed a young German instructor pilot brought a fourth aircraft. The Russian general apparently was amazed that we thought two spares were necessary, and requested a third Tornado flight for his squadron commander. I was told to start briefing with the help of the defence interpreter team. Then the RAF air vice-marshal in charge put his head round the door with a "Sorry, but your station

Author posing with a Sukhoi Su-27 from the Russian air force which was used by their aerobatic team, the Russian Knights.

Members of the Russian air force stood in front of a Sukhoi Su-27.

commander has refused to authorise you". No surprises there then. (Remember the French speaker?) I carried on.

Ten minutes later the AVM looked in and said, "I have no idea how this happened, but you have been personally authorised by the Chief of the Air Staff, who wishes you a pleasant flight." This was the same very senior officer who had posted me to Jever, now several ranks advanced, but still paying his dues. What a man. In the event the flight was a triumph. We agreed to call each other Al and Volodja and I had 12 useful things to say written for me in phonetics. For example, 'I have control' and 'you have control'. In the event, the only Russian phrases needed were 'slow down', 'go up' and 'automatic' when terrain-following radar was engaged. 'I have control' was immediately shortened to 'Al, pilot' when he would sit and sulk, then 'Volodja, pilot' when he would grab the stick once again. Since then, of course, Russian air force air show displays have become legendary. Like the RAF Lightning pilots who yearned for the days of the Lightning F.1, he carried the same nostalgia for the early MiG-21 "before it was overloaded with more fuel tanks".

Close up the Su-27 was really not so nice. It was held together with massive titanium protruding rivets which must have had a vast drag penalty. The engines, however, were enormous, for which I suppose the fuel consumption must have been high. We were offered one spare back seat on the solo display aircraft's practice. Our wing commander won and regretted it. "We spent 15 minutes in a 7-G turn. You would not have liked it." Bryan had a great day chatting to the Russians through the interpreters, but Cottesmore wanted the aircraft back for night flying. At one point an interpreter was not instantly available and an incredibly smooth, well-dressed and good-looking Russian air force pilot stepped forward, "Perhaps I could be of assistance". With immaculate English, he had to be KGB. "I gather that you were formerly a North Sea Phantom pilot." How did he know? I agreed. "Then perhaps we have met before." Volodja was livid and shouted at him for a few minutes until a British interpreter appeared.

As we were leaving, I remembered something else that I wanted to tell my Russian. "Volodja," I started. An interpreter appeared immediately and I noticed that it was the red-tabbed colonel. The translation was seamless as I explained, "My son is 16 and he's studying Russian. What do you think of that?" "My son is 15 and he's studying English." He gripped my arm, and the perfect simultaneous translation came straight through, literally, "When our sons meet, they won't need an arsehole like this." The poor old colonel had translated faultlessly. I asked him how that made

Author with Lieutenant Colonel Bazenov post-GR.1 flight.

him feel. "Well slightly obsolete and frankly a bit of an arsehole." There was no response to that, so we went home.

For me the Cold War ended at that point.

It was 1992 and the UK was slipping into a depression. The CEO of a Peterborough engineering company, to whom I was trying to sell shared flight services said on the phone: "You have totally convinced me that it would be vastly cheaper for me to send out engineers around Europe in a light aircraft. This morning though I just laid off 70 good people. How can I possibly take on an aircraft?" That was the end of the light aircraft project. I was lucky though, a fellow AEF pilot offered me a job on a start-up airline. Yuck! Me an airline pilot? But my head was turned when I found out that I could be flying the A320, a then new fly-by-wire Airbus. In fact, I left the RAF at midnight on terminal leave and halfway through Airbus training, in a late-night café in Toulouse, when a waiter came out to see what the British ''ooligans' were making so much noise about. "He just became a civilian!" He clapped his hands. "Messieurs, we 'ave a procedure for this". The waiter then re-appeared with a massive jug of beer, "Compliments of the direction[12]". I was a civilian once again, and I'd moved on.

Never look back. The next 15 years were fantastic and I travelled the world.

12 French management.

APPENDIX

SIXTY YEARS SAFE

Fighter, airline and glider pilot Alan Munro looks back at sixty years of flight safety.

GASCo Magazine Autumn 2019

As I write this, it is sixty years ago to the day that my ex-RAF instructor got out of the Tiger Moth saying, "One circuit lad, then pick me up here". There was no radio at all at Fairoaks in 1959, so the signal to all that here was an idiot on his first solo was the instructor taking his cushion and standing with it on his head. The flying scholarship was massive fun; we worked hard at the PPL academics, but I really don't remember anyone mentioning safety at all. Yet no one crashed or even caught a finger hand-swinging (except for the mechanic swinging an Edgar Percival E.P.9's three-bladed prop for the first time), so how was it done?

When civil aviation started up again after the Second World War, the vast majority of pilots had been in military service, and we even had ex-national service instructors. All we had to understand was that leadership and airmanship solved most problems, and even in the 1960s when I started to instruct, all lessons began with these two topics. You did as you were told, planned for the worst and hoped for the best. And, of course, we all knew that half the wartime fatalities were in accidents. Nobody except the widows, including my own mother, seemed to mind too much; it was the price of winning. When I was flying my Moth, the RAF was losing Meteors at a colossal rate; causing even Churchill to take note, but that was the unstated price of flying. I should add that the previous year on my cadet gliding course at Hornchurch, the approach was identical.

Your GASCo[13] editor discovered that in those 60 years I had been an RAF flight safety officer (Phantoms at Coningsby), then later an airline FSO (the A320 with Excalibur if you can remember them) and finally as a gliding club safety officer (Buckminster GC at Saltby). I was given little choice in the matter, but at least the airline paid a small amount for the extra work. I also ran a quality and safety business for some 15 years, the brief was to write about the differences between military, civil and gliding safety, and how things had changed over those 60 years. No pressure.

My first tour was flying the Javelin with 60 Squadron at Tengah in Singapore. We certainly enjoyed strong leadership. There was little sympathy to be had if things went wrong, but we had a well-thought-out set of orders and procedures, and we were well trained in jungle and sea survival. The occasional aircraft did crash, and the crew sometimes died. We all went to the funeral and had a great party afterwards. Close ranks and carry on. The navy, whose accident rate was worse than ours, summed it up in the 'Sea Vixen Song' – "Dust to Dust / Ashes to Ashes, / We all get pissed and another one crashes." This was not so much a cavalier attitude as a coping mechanism. It was another form of survival, I think. Britain was still a strong proud nation, and we were its warrior caste.

Even when my navigator and I flew back to Singapore from Gong Kedah on the Thai border, the flight plan was never passed, our radio failed (we had an emergency back-up), and we ended up diverting into Paya Lebar (aka Singapore Civil), under a stack of airliners and between two giant thunderstorms. Everyone thought it was hilarious. My nav's only worry – quite rightly – was that the coconuts on the floor of his cockpit might explode as we climbed to cross an airway at 46,000 ft.

After the Second World War, there were a vast number of small air operators, generally flying surplus aircraft with ex-service pilots. The Dragon Rapide, Anson and Dakota were favourites. There were many accidents, some from poor maintenance and others from trying to set up a new, inadequately regulated industry in British weather. The pilot usually got the blame, but aircraft were comparatively easy to repair. The Chicago Convention and International Civil Aviation Organization (ICAO) were new concepts as governments tried with varying success to regulate this exciting new industry. My mother worked in the Ministry of Civil Aviation at the time, and I remember her saying that accidents were simply the price of commercial flying.

In fact, Ernest Gann describes in *Fate is the Hunter* how he arrived at the west coast of South America with little fuel in a Lockheed Lodestar. If he turned the right way

---

13 General Aviation Safety Council – nothing to do with fast jets but very relevant to the period covered by this book.

there would be an airfield, and the wrong way would bring certain death. He got it right, but it made the point that safety was – at times – literally a 50/50 bet.

Possibly the first airliner accident that really impacted on public consciousness in the UK was the Airspeed Ambassador crash at a snow-covered Munich Airport in 1958 while carrying the victorious 'Busby Babes' home from Belgrade. More than half of the passengers were killed. The cause (an underpowered aircraft trying to take off from an inadequately cleared slush-covered runway) was overlooked in favour of the perennial 'pilot error' (failing to clear ice off the wings) although the captain was exonerated ten years later. Every advance in airliner capability brings new previously unknown problems. For example, the Comet losses, the Boeing 727 flying into Mount Teide in Tenerife and the Airbus A330 diving into the South Atlantic. Each of these accidents was the result of a major technical advance bringing unknown hazards.

More than 50 years ago D. P. Davies, chief test pilot of the UK Air Registration Board, wrote *Handling the Big Jets*. In this seminal work, he suggested that in the future airline pilots should have access to simple aerobatic aircraft to maintain handling skills, with a raw instrument flight once every six months in something like an HS-125. It's never happened – with the honourable exception of South African Airways while they still had Harvards – and although the excellence of modern simulators is great for honing a pilot's instrument skills, do many airlines let their pilots fly 'raw data' (even in the sim) or is the emphasis on correct use of the automatics?

In the air-defence business, we used to regard the ground as the only weapon with a 100 per cent probability of kill. You must, at some stage, learn fear.

What of general aviation (GA) and especially gliding? Initially, GA aircraft were comparatively simple wood and fabric structures, not cheap to build but affordable to repair. The safety record culture was really not too different. A local gliding club used a reverse auto tow around a pulley and had three fatalities after the wire broke. Even at my cadet gliding school (614 VGS, RAF Hornchurch), spin training in the T31 was started at 900 ft AGL, because that was as high as the winch could take you. These days you'd never initiate a spin that low, but a K21 is a very different machine from a T21.

Even in the 1970s risks could be taken that would be unacceptable and possibly illegal today. In 1970, we started night flying at Shobdon with flares made from gallon paint tins half full of sand and a few pints of diesel. When a student pilot was overdue after dithering on his land away cross-country, we got him back in the dark, on this occasion with car lights providing the flare path. Gliders were difficult to rig; mistakes were made and accidents were all too common.

Really, for the first half of the last 60 years, attitudes to safety changed little, while design, training, operations and regulation all improved dramatically. In the 1990s, however, the RAF suffered the Nimrod R1 ditching in the Moray Firth, which moved fear of death to fear of career, and in the civil world JAR-OPS[14] arrived, along with detailed studies of the human factors involved. I never heard human factors mentioned as such until I joined Excalibur. It focussed on the Mount Teide B727 and seemed to be an overstatement of the obvious.

However, in 1994 we had a serious incident where some rushed, unscheduled servicing, (a slat replacement), almost caused an accident. A spoiler popped out in flight and the pilot very nearly lost control getting the aircraft back into Gatwick. The AAIB ruled that it was an engineering error, but behind that lay a chain of management mistakes, including Airbus design and training. It was acknowledged that pretty well everyone goes to work intending to do a good job and that negligence is very rare. It clearly identified the accident chain so that behind the traditional pilot or engineer error, there was a whole line of failures leading to the inevitable accident trigger. The engineer was fined but kept his job.

In 1997 Professor James Reason, a former professor of psychology at Manchester University, wrote his game-changing book called *Managing the Risks of Organisational Accidents*. From this came the now famous 'Swiss Cheese' model in which a hazard comes up against layers of defences (e.g. training, equipment, procedures etc.). If it manages to get through these, there is a consequent loss. The layers were then compared to a Swiss cheese, and you don't always know where the holes are. It's when the holes line up that the hazard gets through and the accident or loss happens. This is now so well accepted by many that at Saltby it's not unusual that when pressure starts to back up someone will say something like: "Hold it. The holes in the cheese are starting to line up." Yes, it's valid for all flying machines, be it a Boeing 747, a Cessna 152 or an F-35.

The introduction of JAR-OPS scared the airlines badly with its quality system, actually a form of self-regulation by which the operator had to keep checking its own processes and doing something about measured failures. This was a dramatic shift from management being told by the CAA inspector what to do. It was inevitably linked in to ISO 9001, the quality standard by which the operator would inevitably have to look at areas like the control of the sub-contractor, while all the regulator needed to see was regulatory compliance. This led to untold arguments about quality

14 JAR-OPS was an interim set of requirements from ICAO working towards standardised European regulation.

versus safety when in fact both are critical business processes for an operator. The engineers were quite unfazed by it all, and the certificatory authority congratulated us on finally catching up. Some operators did indeed use the new disciplines for business enhancement, especially amongst the low-cost operators, and the results show to this day.

Compliance and self-regulation found their way into all parts of EASA, and the MoD mirrored this with the creation of its Military Aviation Authority. In fact, the RAF has moved to a safety centre, I quote: "A safety organisation which delivers effective total safety management and leads on intelligent application of critical thinking. To provide independent assurance of the RAF safety management system underpinning the Chief of Air Staff's commitment to total safety in order to maximise the delivery of RAF capability." The RAF has boldly gone where civil aviation has just fallen short, combining all aspects of safety. Health and safety? No problem. It's just another key business process to be managed. I just hope that leadership and airmanship have not been forgotten.

Safety management has percolated down through commercial aviation into GA. Accountability is achieved though specified management positions, usually approved by the CAA. Even at flying club level, it is pretty well understood that when something is discovered to have gone wrong, there are three courses of action.

- Do nothing. When the cost of the cure overwhelms the cost of the loss;
- Remedial Action. The 'Band-Aid' solution to get by for now;
- Corrective Action. To remove the root cause of the problem.

There is a fourth though, the goal of all safety departments, right down to the gliding club safety officer. Preventive action is taken when we have evidence from auditing, incident reports and regulatory oversight, that it would be pound foolish not to take some form of prophylactic action. At Saltby we recently spent a fortune on the EuroFox, when there were subtle indications that the engine was sub-optimum. A loss of power at low level while towing a glider could cause a nasty accident, so although the engine was still within its TBO (time between overhauls) the club changed it anyway.

The British Gliding Association (BGA), along with the Light Aircraft Association, the British Microlight Aircraft Association and others are at the bottom of the regulatory stack. The BGA, however, has taken upon itself to be the air operator in EASA terms, with the key nominated posts of accountability and responsibility (accountable manager and post holders for maintenance, training and operations, along with a quality manager). However, while each club in regulatory terms is an integral part of the BGA, the chairman is automatically post holder for the club. That's where it gets interesting.

The club managers, like all other GA clubs, now have a statuary responsibility for a safe operation. The BGA does a great job pushing risk awareness and risk avoidance into the clubs but I hear too many CFIs and club safety officers saying that their own management doesn't really understand. At Saltby I enjoy fantastic support from our chairman and board, but on the other hand I use all the tools at my disposal, including a mini safety-management system, to present a safety action plan to every board meeting. We have records of management actions on safety going back nearly five years now so that we can demonstrate that risk is 'as low as reasonably practicable' (ALARP). If there's a weakness it may be the fierce independence of the average glider pilot not caring for too much oversight. Sadly a new CFI with innate self-belief as a safety expert did not buy and the club safety-management system collapsed.

What else has changed? I suppose that in the gliding world the iron hand of the insurance companies is not far away. The cost and frequency of glider repairs have rocketed to the point where the very sport is threatened. We must do better to bring these costs and damage down.

Have I answered the task? 'What are the safety differences and similarities between the disciplines, and what's changed over the years?' I hope so. The unasked question must be 'What have I learned?' Put simply it's that 'you don't know what you don't know'. It took a while to find that out, but that's what modern safety is all about, working out what you don't know and then doing something about it before the holes in the cheese line up.

GLOSSARY

2ATAF	Second Allied Tactical Air Force
4ATAF	Fourth Allied Tactical Air Force
AAFCE	Allied Air Forces Central Europe
AAR	Air-to-Air Refuelling
ADIZ	Air Defence Identification Zone
AEF	Air Experience Flight
AEW	Airborne Early Warning
ANG	Air National Guard (US)
APC	Armament Practice Camp
ATAF	Allied Tactical Air Force
AWACS	Airborne Warning and Control System
CFS	Central Flying School
DACT	Dissimilar Air Combat Training
DAW	Department of Air Warfare
ECM	Electronic Countermeasures
FAW	Fighter All Weather
FGR	Fighter employed in Ground Attack or Reconnaissance
FIR	Flight Information Region
GAF	German Air Force
IFF	Indentification Friend or Foe
IGB	Inner German Border
INAS	Inertial Navigation and Attack System
IP	Instructor Pilot
MoD	Ministry of Defence

NAFFI	Naval, Army and Air Force Institute
NBC	Nuclear, Biological and Chemical
NCO	Non-Commissioned Officer
Oberst	Colonel
Oberstleutnant	German Lieutenant Colonel
OCU	Operational Conversion Unit
Offizierheim	German Officers' Mess
Ostmark	Basic monetary unit of the German Democratic Republic
PK	Probability of Kill
QFI	Qualified Flying Instructor
QRA	Quick Reaction Alert
RAFG	Royal Air Force Germany
Recce	Reconnaissance
SAM	Surface-to-Air Missile
Stadtdirektor	Town Clerk
SFSO	Station Flight Safety Officer
TACAN	Tactical Air Navigation System
TLP	Tactical Leadership Programme
TTTE	Tornado Tri-National Training Establishment
UHF	Ultra-High Frequency
Volkssturm	'People's Militia' a Nazi group from WWII
VOPO	*Volkspolizei* (police force of the German Democratic Republic)

INDEX